My Life with Hatti

My Life
with
Hatti

Six Years With A Dog Who
Does Everything

LIBBY
CLEGG

Quercus

First published in Great Britain in 2021 by Quercus.

Quercus Editions Ltd
Carmelite House
50 Victoria Embankment
London EC4Y 0DZ

An Hachette UK company

A CIP catalogue record for this book is available
from the British Library

HB ISBN 978 1 52941 667 1
TPB ISBN 978 1 52941 668 8
Ebook ISBN 978 1 52941 670 1

PICTURE CREDITS

All images are © and courtesy of the author except, in order of appearance:
5 (Cameron Spencer/Getty Images), 6 (Julian Finney/Getty Images),
7 (Atsushi Tomura/Getty Images), 9 (Lucas Uebel/Getty Images),
12 (Mike Marsland/WireImage)

10 9 8 7 6 5 4 3 2 1

Typeset by CC Book Production
Printed and bound in Great Britain by Clays Ltd, Elcograf S.p.A.

Papers used by Quercus Editions Ltd. are from well-managed forests
and other responsible sources.

Behind every athlete there is a group of people who help deliver the performances we see at the Paralympic Games, and this is the same for each and every Guide Dog.

I'd like to dedicate this book to all of the volunteers at Guide Dogs. Without them my life and many others wouldn't be the same. Having Hatti has empowered me in every way.

Most of all I would like to thank Zoe Hamilton-Wynne and Debbie Edwards for the integral role they played in Hatti's early life. To Zoe for the incredible work she has done as a puppy raiser and Debbie for the patience and dedication it took to put Hatti through her advanced training.

Contents

INTRODUCTION

The inspiration for me wanting to write a book about my unorthodox life with a beautiful Labrador/Retriever cross has come from everywhere really: my family, athletics, ice dancing! They all form part of the story you are about to read, and the first two in particular have been essential elements.

By far my biggest inspiration, though, has been a yearning to tell as many people as possible, not just how amazing guide dogs like Hatti are, but how important they are to people like me. Without her, my life over the past six years wouldn't have been anywhere near as happy, fun or fulfilling as it has been. I'm probably a better person too, although that's not really for me to decide.

There's a famous saying I've heard that goes, 'You don't always know what you've got till it's gone.' In my case, I didn't know what I had until Hatti arrived. All of a sudden life opened up for me and the fact that we've experienced the vast majority of what's gone on since then together has been the icing on the cake. Friend, confidant, companion, therapist! Guide dogs don't just guide people geographically, they can help them emotionally too. Sometimes by appearing to empathise, which I think they do, in their own way, and sometimes just by being there. I don't want to spoil the story but there have been several times in my recent life where, more than anything else in the world, I've needed somebody who is just there by my side. Somebody I can talk to, cry my eyes out in front of and hug. But also somebody who *I* am responsible for. If it was all about what Hatti could do for me then it wouldn't be a partnership, would it, and that's the definition of what we have. A partnership. She's dedicated to me, and I to her. It'll be the same the world over with people who have helping dogs, you mark my words.

One thing I didn't realise when I first applied for a guide dog was the fact that they're available in so few countries. I know it's a cliché but we take so much for granted these days and I'm guilty of having assumed that they were everywhere. If only! In fact, only thirty-one countries have guide-dog schools at the moment so there's an awful long way to go.

In some countries there is obviously a cultural barrier and the chances of there ever being guide dogs in some of these places are slim. As sad as that might be, there are plenty of countries in the world that would welcome a guide-dog programme with open arms and I'm happy to report that, slowly but surely, the word is finally spreading. Let me give you an example.

A few years ago I met a lady called Maggie Moore who is the

wife of the then British Ambassador to Turkey, Richard Moore. Maggie is visually impaired and has a guide dog and after moving over to Turkey she helped to set up a guide-dog association with some locals. There are roughly 800,000 registered blind people living independently in Turkey and now some of them will have guide dogs. Not many, but as word continues to grow, so, hopefully, will the association.

The problem you have isn't just how a country perceives or treats dogs, it's also down to things like hygiene. The only place in the UK where I'm not allowed to take Hatti is an intensive care unit, but that kind of access hasn't just appeared overnight. It's taken a long time and a lot of hard work by a lot of people. Now imagine having to start again from scratch and in a country where dogs are viewed very differently to here. That's the task that people like Maggie have ahead of them, not to mention things like setting up breeding programmes and training schools.

By far the best advert for having more guide dogs in a country that isn't necessarily known as b

eing dog friendly is seeing them in action, so the more there are on the streets helping people, the more likely the public are to accept them. Another success story is South Africa, which, despite having had a guide-dogs charity there since 1953, has made huge strides over the past few years and now has a national charity that is thriving. I actually went to train there a few years ago and one morning while I was in the gym a Paralympic athlete walked in with a guide dog. According to the athlete, guide dogs were still as rare as hen's teeth in the country and the fact that they'd managed to get one had made an incredible difference to their life. It was a beautiful dog, by the way.

Back in the UK, one of the things there's a shortage of at the moment is puppy trainers. Puppy trainers are basically the primary school teachers of the guide-dog world and play a vital role in their early socialisation and education. In fact, if that period isn't successful the dogs can't go into training, so it's essential. Hatti's puppy trainer, Debbie, has a fantastic track record of getting dogs into training and so that's what we need – more Debbies! The charity are definitely looking for volunteers though, so if you'd like more information please visit the volunteering section at www.guidedogs.org.uk. Anyone can volunteer and it's obviously great fun. That's my first and last appeal, I promise!

Whether it be a guide dog and a blind person or a hearing dog and a deaf person, each partnership will be unique yet they will all be based on exactly the same principles. Namely, trust, loyalty, understanding and love. These amazing animals are so much more than eyes and ears. They are the difference between happiness and sadness, confidence and shyness, can and can't. Even life and death, sometimes. They are *the difference*.

I really hope you enjoy the book.

Libby Clegg – Loughborough 2021

CHAPTER ONE

THIS IS ME

Every dog/human relationship will have its own unique story. Involving one of the planet's most beloved animals – that's definitely dogs, by the way – these stories tend to be heavy on things like loyalty and affection and will usually begin with one or both parties becoming smitten during the first meeting. Ring any bells? I could be wrong, but I'd hazard a guess that love at first sight is far more common between dogs and humans than it is between humans and humans or even dogs and dogs. I've lost count of the number of times I've been with friends who arrive home only to shout a cursory 'Hiya!' to their preoccupied partners and children before engaging in a joyous five-minute reunion with their dog. It's actually really touching as it's always completely genuine.

The relationships between guide dogs and the people they help begin differently and are usually forged from things like necessity and trust as opposed to love. That comes later, although

I know from personal experience that over time, these relationships can transcend the norm and grow into something special and unique. Hence this book. You'll also get things like denial thrown into the mix occasionally – on the part of the human who might not think they need a guide dog – which can complicate things. Pairing a guide dog with a human is rarely straightforward, but then nobody said it would be.

Mine and Hatti's relationship came about because I needed help, although it took me quite a long time to admit it, which is why I mention denial. I'm certainly not the first person who's registered blind to be in denial about needing help and I definitely won't be the last. I also won't be the only one who, while slowly coming to terms with this fact, ended up making a fool of themself.

My own denial was nothing more than a prolonged bout of stubbornness, really, culminating in a fight at about ten o'clock one night between me and some nicely manicured topiary. Yes, you read that correctly: topiary. But before I tell you about that, we need to go back a bit further. I think they call it 'the backstory'.

I was born in 1990 and spent the first few years of my life in a little village in Cheshire called Bollington. I'm the eldest of four children – I have a sister called Felicity who was born in 1992 and two brothers, James and Stephen, who were born in 1994 and 1995, respectively – and all in all, we had a pretty calm and idyllic childhood.

A question I'm often asked is whether I come from sporting stock, and here I always have to disappoint. My mum was ok at sport when she was at school but that's about the extent of it, I'm afraid. I wouldn't say my forebears were inactive, as such. They just weren't very sporty.

What's funny is that despite my ancestors not showing much in the way of sporting prowess, my brothers, James and Stephen, have, which makes three out of four from one generation. We're like buses really. Nobody shows any interest for generations and then three come along at once! They too are Paralympic athletes (they're both swimmers) and in addition to James winning bronze in the men's S12 100m butterfly at the 2012 London Paralympics, Stephen, who made his Paralympic debut at Rio in 2016, won a silver medal at the World Para Swimming Championships in 2019 and recently broke the S12 100m butterfly world record. Out of all of us Stephen's the one with the most athletic physique. He's 6ft 4in. and has massive feet like flippers, whereas James and I are shorter and are what you might call less genetically gifted. I have to say it was lovely having James with me for London 2012 and Stephen in Rio for 2016. All being well, Stephen will be with me in Tokyo in 2021 if it goes ahead. Fingers crossed!

My dad was the first person to notice that there might be a problem with my sight. I was about six or seven at the time and my sister, Felicity, who is twenty-two months younger than me, was starting to catch me up in the reading stakes. To be honest, I don't think he was sure that it was my sight, he just knew there was a problem. I was completely oblivious to all of this, as any six- or seven-year-old would be.

The first time *I* realised that something might be wrong was in

1998. I'd just moved up to a new class at school and I remember struggling to read what was on the whiteboard. To compound the problem, I was the only girl in the group I'd been put into within the class, and asking the boys for help wasn't going to happen. They were appalled at having a girl in their group and I was *persona non grata* from day one. Worse still, our teacher was about as approachable as an angry bull, so basically, I had to think up ways of getting closer to the whiteboard without getting shouted at. The work we had to do was always written on there, so it was essential.

'Miss, can I go to the loo please?'

'What, again? That's the third time today!'

It was horrible.

It got so bad with this teacher that I ended up having to move schools. I won't divulge too many details, but when I found out I was leaving, it was a massive relief. My new school was much bigger and my new teacher far less scary. Even so, I still felt uneasy about asking for help, so I squinted my way through the first few weeks via visits to the loo.

I'm not sure what triggered it exactly, but one day, my new teacher asked to see my mum and told her that she thought I needed an eye test. I first went to see an optometrist who gave me a pair of glasses which, to be fair, improved my focus slightly. In my eyes (pardon the pun), this was all I needed as the glasses prevented me from having to ask for help so much. All kids want to do is fit in, especially at school, and that was all I was bothered about.

Within a few weeks though, my eyesight was back to square one again and after I'd owned up to my parents and teacher that things had got worse, I was referred to the Manchester Royal Eye Hospital, where I ended up having lots of tests over a period of weeks. Again, the thing that bothered me wasn't the fact that my eyesight was a bit dodgy (it was my central vision that was failing) – it was the fact that I was different to all the other kids. The only upside was the hospital waiting room, which had every toy imaginable. Sometimes, I'd be there for five or six hours and I remember being called from there to have a test and feeling gutted. It was always when I was having the most fun.

I dread to think how many tests I had in all but in the end, I was diagnosed with Stargardt's macular dystrophy, or Stargardt's disease, as it's more commonly known – an inherited single-gene retinal disease that can start in childhood, adolescence or adulthood and results in a progressive loss of vision. I remember sitting in the consultation room with my parents and the doctor who diagnosed me. While he was busy trying to explain to Mum and Dad what the disease was, and the prognosis with regards to my eyesight, I was getting very bored indeed, as most children would. It was all gobbledygook to me and all I wanted to do was get back to the waiting room and continue my game.

A few days later, my mum sat me down and tried to explain it all to me. The majority of what she said went over my head (either that or I wasn't listening), but what's still very vivid is her trying to explain to me that I was going to be registered blind and would be classed as being disabled. That's when it started to hit home, I think, although I remember being very confused at the time. To me, being disabled meant being in a wheelchair and I wasn't in a wheelchair. I just couldn't see very well. Mum also tried explaining to me that my eyesight would eventually get worse, which again went completely over my head. My eyesight was still ok and at that age, until something actually happens, it just doesn't seem real.

All I could think about after our conversation was the fact that I was going to be disabled yet didn't need a wheelchair. In fact, as far as I was concerned, I had next to nothing wrong with me. How could I be disabled if I was fit and healthy? Nothing at all made sense.

The people who were affected most by this, at least initially, were my parents. They were absolutely devastated. They've never told me this, but because the disease is inherited I'm pretty sure that they both felt responsible. And although that's a perfectly natural reaction, the very thought of my parents feeling responsible for my condition almost brings me to tears. There's no history of it in my family prior to me, so how on earth could they have known?

The doctor told my parents that there was a one in four chance of their children developing the disease. With three other children all younger than me, this obviously put them on tenterhooks. Sadly, about a year later, my brother James was diagnosed with the disease and a few years after that Stephen was too. James and I have brown hair and Felicity and Stephen are blond, so when James and I were diagnosed, my parents made a link and assumed it would stop there. For years, they were told that Stephen would be ok, so when he was eventually diagnosed, they took it very badly. The odds were that it should have stopped with me, and as hopeful parents, they'd probably been banking on it. Unfortunately, odds like that are not an exact science.

When I was first diagnosed, I felt like the odd one out and I have to admit that when James was diagnosed it made me feel less so. I'd never have wished it on him, but my reasoning was that at least he'd have an ally in me and I in him. This came into its own as we got older and more independent. We were a team almost, pushed together by the fact that we could each understand the other's predicament and help one another out. When Stephen was eventually diagnosed, he became part of that team and the unfortunate upshot of that was that Felicity felt like the odd one out. She also felt guilty for being the only one who didn't have the disease, which was sad. For a time, we were all at each other's throats, but then what family isn't?

Now we're all grown up, things have improved and even though my brothers and I do have a link through our condition, we make up for it in other ways with Felicity. For instance, I often have trouble reading labels on packets of food and whenever that happens, I'll take a photo and send it to Felicity with a series of questions. She's so helpful and has prevented me from getting food poisoning on more than one occasion. 'For God's sake, don't eat that,' she'll say. 'It's a year past its sell-by date!'

She's also great at things like grammar and emails and has often made me sound a lot more intellectual than I am!

When I went back to school after being diagnosed, I had to work one-to-one with a classroom assistant, which blew the whole 'fitting-in' thing completely out of the water. Next, they got me a stand which raised my books and papers closer to my face and instead of a pencil, I had to use a thick felt-tip pen. Whenever the teacher printed anything out for the class, she had to do separate sheets for me and everything had to be in a size 48 font. The problem we had there was that the more you enlarge something on a photocopier the more it fades, so while it was always big, it was sometimes almost invisible. Worst of all, every enlarged sheet was a reminder that I was the odd one out in a class of about thirty, and the older I got, the worse this became.

To be fair to the school, and to my classmates, everyone was really helpful, so it could have been a lot worse. You hear some real horror stories about kids who have a disability of some kind being bullied or ignored and I never experienced anything like that. Nothing was too much trouble for the school, and I was even given the chance to have touch-typing lessons which helped me a lot.

Unfortunately, things changed dramatically when I went to secondary school. Every single one of my friends was going to be attending the local Catholic school which was obviously where I wanted to go. They didn't have the support in place to take someone like me though, which meant I had to go to a much larger school that could accommodate individual needs. Since the diagnosis, my school friends had become my support network and losing them was very difficult. All the cruelty and isolation I hadn't had to suffer at primary school, partly thanks to them, suddenly appeared overnight and I went from enjoying school to absolutely hating it. My form class were ok, but the moment I left that environment, I became a target. I don't think I'd met many older children prior to going to secondary school and I was shocked at how cruel they could be. I still am in a way. I kind of get how kids behave sometimes, but what on earth would make you want to be nasty to somebody who needs help?

Had I taken the same classes as the other children, things might have been different, but I was forever being taken out of class to do 'blind person' things such as Braille. This, although essential for my future, was just another reminder to everybody that I was different. I was also the only pupil in my year who required any kind of help, so there were no allies to be had or friends to be made on that basis.

The ultimate ignominy was when I had to start using a white cane. This was the final nail in the coffin as far as school was concerned, and I went from being somebody who was often isolated, occasionally mocked and barely tolerated, to somebody who was completely ignored by everyone. Even some of the teachers weren't terribly keen. I was quite good at maths and I was put in the top set, but my teacher didn't want the hassle of having to deal with me, so I was moved to the bottom set instead. This ended up being a blessing in disguise, as instead of me having to endure that old battleaxe week in, week out I now had a teacher who, as well as being quite kind to me, made sure I was given the correct level of work. There were also a couple of classroom assistants who were very nice. Both were called Mrs Watson; one was known to the kids as Curly Mrs Watson and the other Spiky Mrs Watson, obviously down to their hair. They did me the honour of simply speaking to me as you would to any other child and I'll always be grateful for that.

Fortunately, this hell only lasted one year (it seemed like ten) because in 2002, my parents decided to move up to the Scottish Borders. This, for all kinds of reasons, was a dream move for me, not least because instead of having to take my chances at a comprehensive school, which may or may not have been an improvement on the last place, I was enrolled at the Royal Blind School in Edinburgh. The Royal Blind School is residential (unless you live nearby, I suppose) and, as the name suggests, the children who attend are all visually impaired. It was amazing being there. Almost overnight, I went from being a pariah to being, dare I say it, normal. Despite us all having slightly different needs, everybody supported each other as a matter of course and the atmosphere was diametrically opposed to the one I'd been used to. The class sizes too were tiny – I don't think we ever had more than eight in a class while I was there. Don't get me wrong, we certainly had disagreements on occasion. We were kids, after all. We all had something in common though, which ultimately bonded us together.

Being away from home from Monday to Friday was a bit scary at first, but the relief of being around people who faced the same issues I did, day to day, knocked that out of the ball park. It was like going from a country where you don't speak the language to one where you're fluent. But it wasn't just the people. The work, for instance, was all pre-prepared specifically for us, so there was no photocopying sheets of A4 paper in a 48 font and then worrying if you'd be able to see them or not. The computers also had appropriate technology installed on them, which I wasn't used to.

Since starting to lose my sight, I'd had to fit into a world that wasn't designed for people who were visually impaired and it had never even occurred to me that there might be one that was. Many of the lessons at the school were geared towards helping us live independently, so there was a big emphasis on things like home economics. That subject was compulsory, and I remember my first lesson as if it were yesterday. We were taught how to make a cup of tea in the microwave! I suppose it sounds daft, but kettles are to be avoided if you can't see very well, and with drinking tea in our house almost mandatory, this made perfect sense! After that, we went on to cooking with a few bog-standard meals and we were also taught how to clean up after ourselves. Most twelve- or thirteen-year-old children would probably balk at this kind of thing, but it gave us all some confidence. It was the same with things like laundry. Because the school was residential, we had to take care of our own sheets and things, so the overall effect, while slightly unconventional for kids of our age, was actually quite empowering. How many thirteen-year-olds do you know who can run a household?

The only part of the whole independent living thing that I wasn't keen on was being taught how to use a white cane. This was part of what they called mobility classes and I absolutely loathed it. This probably sounds ridiculous coming from some-body who is registered blind, but the reason I hated using a cane (and still do) is because it makes you look like somebody who – well, is registered blind! You're probably thinking, hang on a minute, what about a guide dog? They don't exactly scream, 'Look, she's fully sighted.' There is a difference though, which I'll come to shortly.

Unfortunately, we weren't allowed to leave the school without a white cane, so if you included the mobility classes, which generally took place outside the school, they were pretty ubiq-uitous. Canes aside though, the mobility classes could be quite fun sometimes and included having to get yourself to certain destinations in and around Edinburgh. The first one I remember having to master, when I was twelve, was the route from the school to a well-known medical bookshop. Why they chose that place I have no idea, but after negotiating that route, I had to find my way to a well-known Chinese takeaway and after that a well-known shop and bakery. Each trip was equivalent to a pass, and the more passes you notched up (you had to meet somebody at the destination to prove you'd done it), the further you were allowed to go. Not just during classes, but during your free time also.

The more challenging trips would require you having to ask for help or information and might include a ride on a train and a bus or two. Once again, this was all about building confidence and becoming independent, and despite the white cane, I really enjoyed it. It could be quite scary at times, but that's all part and parcel. The more times you do something, the more natural it becomes, and by the time I was fifteen, I could get from one end of Edinburgh to the other with my eyes closed. Not that that would have made a great deal of difference!

One of my first big-ish trips was from the blind school, which is in an area called Cameron Toll, Craigmillar Park, to the Gyle Shopping Centre, five or six miles away in a place called South Gyle. As the crow flies, five or six miles isn't very far, but instead of a crow I had a white stick and instead of open skies, I had a walk to the bus stop, a bus ride to the train station, a train ride to South Gyle and, finally, a very long walk to the shopping centre ahead of me. I don't mind admitting that I was a little bit nervous when I set off, as the final walk from the train station could be quite tricky. It's probably getting on for about half a mile, with lots of other paths leading off and on to it at various points. Several friends of mine had fallen foul of this while making the same journey and had ended up getting lost, so I was super careful. Fortunately, I made it there in one piece, unscathed, and that was probably the catalyst for me becoming – or at least feeling – properly independent. It was like getting my wings, in a way. I still hated the cane though.

On Friday afternoons, I was supposed to get a taxi back home to the Scottish Borders with my brothers James and Stephen, who also attended the school. After going solo to South Gyle, this went out of the window and instead of travelling home with Stephen and James, I'd stay on and train in the gym for a couple of hours and then make my own way home, either to Carlisle by train or to our village by bus. Either was fine with me because I was independent!

In all seriousness though, the only reason I did this was because I genuinely felt confident enough; in that respect, the blind school and the brilliant staff and teachers were worth their weight in gold. If you lose one of your senses, such as sight or hearing, the others will probably compensate to some degree. This is worth nothing though unless you have the confidence to utilise it. Confidence is almost a sixth sense, as it can empower you and enable you to do so much.

Speaking of gyms, I can't believe I haven't talked much about the athletics yet. Silly me! I started running shortly before being officially diagnosed when I was nine. It was Mum's idea and was an attempt at preventing whatever was going on from getting the better of me, while at the same time encouraging me to live as normal a life as possible. She didn't just pluck the idea from thin air though; I was always quite competitive and enjoyed things like sports day, so it seemed logical.

The club I wanted to join was Macclesfield Harriers and before they'd accept me, Mum had to explain what I was going through. Fortunately, they were very understanding and welcomed me with open arms. I'm not saying I was a natural or anything, but I worked hard, and, just like the blind school later on, it both inspired and empowered me. It was also a perfect antidote when things were difficult at my school in Cheshire; all things considered, it probably saved me from getting depressed. You always need something to look forward to in life and when everyone at the comprehensive school was blanking me, I knew I still had friends at the Harriers and would continue to have fun there.

Things started getting serious athletics-wise when I was about fourteen. I got scouted one day when competing at a meeting and was invited to join the world-class development squad at British Athletics which, at the time, was known as UK Athletics. I still didn't really know what all that meant, but I went along with it all the same. I was enjoying myself, so there was no problem.

Something I knew a little bit more about at the time was the Paralympic Games which, when I got scouted, were taking place in Athens. One of the reasons I remember this was because a friend of mine was competing in the marathon at the 2004 Paralympic Games and instead of showing it live on television as I thought they would, the BBC replaced the coverage with a rerun of the previous year's Great North Run. What?! That's one of the first times I can remember getting angry at the tele-vision. I was spitting feathers! The coverage had been pretty bad throughout the Games, so this was the final insult.

As well as making me want to throw things at the TV and strangle someone at the BBC, this experience pushed the Paralympic Games to the forefront of my consciousness, and when all the annoyance and outrage had subsided, I was left with an almost overwhelming desire to get involved. I wanted to be a Paralympian.

Fortunately, my enthusiasm for athletics continued and in 2006, aged sixteen, I was selected to compete at the World Championships in Holland. This was my first major competition and despite almost exploding with excitement when they told me I was going, I was being taken there more as a development athlete so I wouldn't be breaking any records. This fact meant little to me as I was well aware of my age and inexperience. What changed things slightly was when Radio 5 Live referred to me as a potential medal hope for the future. As with those journeys across Edinburgh, this inspired me somewhat and I ended up asking one of my coaches if he agreed with the assessment. 'Mmmmm. Maybe in 2012,' he said slightly dismissively. This too fired something inside me, and I ended up leaving the championships with a silver medal, which I won in the 200m. It should really have been two, but Lincoln – my guide runner at the time – accidentally crossed the line before me in the 100m, so we got disqualified. This happens at least once in every guide's career.

So, between the BBC's patchy coverage of the Paralympic Games, somebody on Radio 5 Live referring to me as a future medal hope and my coach all but dismissing the idea, I had gained enough confidence and motivation to win a silver medal at my first major championships and from there I just kicked on.

But back to the backstory . . .

*

The idea of me getting a guide dog was first mooted back in 2012. It was my parents who suggested it, and initially, I dismissed their proposal outright. It just seemed like a massive hindrance to me and I had no enthusiasm for it whatsoever. This put my parents off for a time, but after a while, they mentioned it again and then other people joined the chorus.

My other reason for not wanting a guide dog was simply that I didn't think I needed one. I was quite happy chuntering along and bumping into things occasionally. Looking back, I think I also had a problem with stigma and association. I still didn't consider myself a partially sighted person. I considered myself a normal person who did things a bit differently. In my mind, getting a guide dog would not only have reminded me that I was partially sighted, but also forced me to associate myself with blind people and, at the time, I wasn't ready for that. You can almost smell the denial, can't you?

I took my refusal to accept the truth into overdrive when I left the blind school, the first thing I did on leaving being to ditch my cane. I'd always hated the blasted thing, but as opposed to treating them as a necessary evil, which is what they actually are (if I'm being rational), I convinced myself that I genuinely didn't need one under any circumstances and so embarked on a ridiculous campaign of self-harm (bumping into things) and assault and criminal damage (bumping into other people and their property).

I remember one of my friends asking me why I refused to use a cane one day.

'Because it makes me look like a flipping blind person!' I answered.

To which they said, 'But you *are* a flipping blind person!'

'No, I'm not,' I replied. 'I'm only partially blind.'

'You're blind enough to keep bumping into things every ten yards,' they said.

The more conversations I had in this vein, the more I dug my heels in, and so it went on. At the end of the day though, I have a degenerative eye condition, so it was only ever going to get worse.

One of the other problems I had with a white cane was the effect they have on the general public. To me, they create a sense of awkwardness that would often result in me being asked a series of questions about how blind I was. The thing is, I still had to ask people for help sometimes and without a white cane or a guide dog I had to tell them about my condition before asking for help. The fact that I had to ask for help in the first place was another massive bone of contention with me, but I just couldn't realise that the whole thing was self-defeating. This came to a rather amusing head one day in my local supermarket. I was after a bag of rice and after getting myself to the correct aisle, I approached somebody about helping me to do the last bit. On this occasion, I decided that I would dispense with the whole, 'Excuse-me-I'm-registered-blind' bit and come straight to the point.

'Excuse me,' I said to the chosen one. 'Could you help me find the white rice please?'

'Forgotten your glasses, have you?'

'Yes,' I said, forcing a laugh. 'I'm afraid I have.'

'Here,' said the man. 'You can borrow these.'

With that, he handed me a pair of thick black-rimmed spectacles, which not only wouldn't have helped me to see, but would also have made me look like Eric Morecambe. It was time to come clean.

'I'm really sorry,' I said. 'I've told you a bit of a lie.' And I ended up having to go through my entire introduction and, because of what had happened, it was twice as long as it might have been. The man was very nice and helpful, which is actually the rule as opposed to the exception. I think I'd forgotten that. It made me think, Do you know what? I don't need to do this any more. People need to know that I have a problem seeing, and nine times out of ten they're happy to help – cane or no cane. On top of this, I'd started bumping into people, and without a cane or a guide dog, I was often accused of being clumsy or ignorant. I'd also had a couple of near misses when I'd almost been hit by a car. It wasn't good. I was a menace!

Without wanting to detract from the point I've been making, I think this might be an ideal time to offer a few examples of some of the more light-hearted incidents that have taken place. At the end of the day, if I couldn't laugh at what goes on I'd spend my entire life being miserable, and that's not me at all.

One of my own personal favourite, 'Oh my God, what on earth have I done?' moments, is when I've got into a stranger's car. The first time it happened was at a train station. I rang a friend about twenty minutes before arriving and she said she'd pick me up outside the front. My friend had a small black car and after emerging through the station doors I spotted one, assumed it was hers, walked up to the passenger door with the aid of my white cane, opened the door, jumped in, closed the door and put the seat belt on. All the time I was happily telling the person in the driving seat, who I assumed was my friend, about my journey and it was only when I came to a halt after putting on the seat belt that I realised what had happened. Fortunately, I couldn't really see the reaction of the driver very well and I didn't hang around to get a better look. They told me not to worry and were very nice but I felt like such a massive idiot!

The worst occasions – so this has happened to me quite a few times, you may have gathered – are when I've done it when I haven't been using either a white cane or a guide dog. Because I don't look blind, to all intents and purposes, the person getting into the stranger's car is a fully sighted human being. Luckily for me I've always been talking at a hundred miles an hour so while it probably does seem quite bizarre, hopefully I'm not too scary or intimidating. I've just come for a chat, basically. In a stranger's car and with a seat belt on!

I have actually done this with Hatti, by the way. Instead of just getting in the front seat, I've opened up the back door, ushered Hatti in, closed the back door, opened up the front door, jumped in, and put my seat belt on. This mistake is obviously a bit easier to understand and is usually met with a, 'Erm, I think you might have the wrong car,' to which I now always reply, 'Oh my God, not again! I'm so sorry.'

What I usually do now is instead of trying to locate the car I ask whoever's giving me a lift to give me a shout. That way at least if I go towards a wrong car they can prevent me getting in!

The only thing that could rival travel when it comes to creating these situations is catering, or more specifically, buffets. Unless I have somebody with me or there's somebody around to help, these can be a disaster and because I'm a fussy eater they usually are! Well, not a disaster, but I always end up either spitting something out or eating something I don't like. I'll give you one example. A few years ago I was competing in Poland and at breakfast one morning there didn't seem to be anyone around at the buffet. No matter, I knew the general direction of what I wanted so carried on. When I sat down, instead of tucking into a nice bowl of fruit salad and pineapple I got a mouthful of Polish cake and dried apricots! Had I carried on eating the dried apricots I would have been running for more than just my country that day! One of the worst experiences I've had is picking up what I assumed was a nice bowl of natural yoghurt before putting a tablespoon of horseradish sauce into my mouth. The shock of it happening was awful but not nearly as bad as the taste. I had to drink about a gallon of water! Why didn't I smell it first? I've also picked up handfuls of scotch bonnet chillies instead of tomatoes at the supermarket, which is interesting.

If we're talking out-and-out embarrassment, the only one that can rival travel is toilets. As well as becoming an expert in getting a guide dog and a human being into cubicles of all sizes, I've also become quite adept at mistaking gents' toilets for ladies' toilets. Like getting into cars, I've done that with Hatti, and without Hatti, and it's definitely worse without Hatti! If it's somewhere I've never been before I'll always try and find the disabled toilet first, but if I can't find one and I'm busting, I just have to take pot luck and hope for the best! Normally I can tell if I've gone to the gents, either by the smell or because there'll be some urinals, but if there aren't any urinals and only cubicles I'm in trouble!

Something I learned early on is not to let the embarrassment of these things get to you. The embarrassment is inevitable sometimes but letting it get to you isn't. The vast majority of people who are on the receiving end of these incidents are kind and understanding and you have to see the funny side. I mean, what's not funny about mistaking scotch bonnet chillies for tomatoes, walking into gents' toilets or getting into a stranger's car with a dog?

Before I move on, there is one more example I'd like to share with you, and that's ignoring people. Not on purpose, of course, but if you can't see somebody waving at you and they don't know you're blind it can cause all kinds of problems. Usually not serious ones, but it always results in some explaining having to be done followed by lots of apologies from both sides. A friend of mine who was at university used to have an apartment in the halls of residence with a window on the ground floor and one day she was stopped by a fellow student. 'Excuse me,' he said. 'I've waved at you every day since the start of term and you haven't waved back once. Have I done something wrong?' He was really nice apparently and genuinely thought he'd upset her. 'I can't see,' said my friend. 'I would have waved back though, if I'd known.'

This happens to me all the time and what I tend to do these days is when I'm getting to know somebody I'll say to them, 'Look, if you see me and wave and I don't wave back, it's not because I'm being rude. I just can't see you.' I hate the thought of somebody thinking I'm being rude, so knowing they won't think that always makes me feel better.

The funniest thing is when somebody comes up to me who I already know but don't recognise. Not because I've forgotten who they are, but because I can't see them properly. Once again, I don't want to appear rude so what I always try and do in this situation is buy myself time by getting them to speak. I recognise voices like some people do faces and nine times out of ten I'll get there. Sometimes my mind will draw a blank unfortunately and in that situation I have to come clean!

By the end of 2013, my eyesight had deteriorated further, yet I was still walking around like somebody who had 20/20 vision. Or a stupid, stubborn idiot, as the majority of people who knew me at the time would have said. Things were put into perspective by my dad who said that if I walked out into the road one day into the path of an oncoming car and that car killed me, the driver would have to live with that for the rest of their lives, yet it would have been my fault, not theirs. This really hit home and left me almost speechless. Putting myself at risk unnecessarily was bad enough, but putting other people at risk so I could fool myself into believing that I wasn't partially sighted was just ridiculous. There was no excuse for it.

The actual catalyst for me deciding to apply for a guide dog came a few days later when I was on my way home from the train station. It was about ten o'clock at night and I was on the phone to my dad. The deal was that whenever I walked anywhere late at night by myself, I'd always ring one of my parents because girls ring home when walking in the dark, with or without eyesight, and on this occasion it was Dad's turn. Lucky him!

I can't think how many times I must have made that journey, but when I was about halfway home I walked straight into a hedge. Not half into it. Straight into it – headlong. 'Are you ok?' asked Dad. 'What's happened?'

'You're not going to believe this,' I said, trying to extract myself from the topiary. 'I've just walked straight into a bloody hedge!' There was then a silence that I knew was my cue to admit it was time to make a change. 'Ok,' I said to Dad. 'You can tell Mum that I'll call the charity tomorrow and apply to get a guide dog.'

'She'll be relieved,' said Dad. 'As will the person whose hedge you've just vandalised! You've made the right decision.'

Dad was right. I had made the right decision. And if I could change anything at all about how I came to it, I'd probably shave a few months off. I know I'm making light of the situation, but accepting you have a disability and then agreeing to ask for help can be difficult, especially when you've worked so hard to be independent. It's not something that comes naturally to me and I think it's the same with a lot of people, especially young people. In fact, one of my other problems with having a guide dog was that I associated them with older people. Not necessarily pensioners, but I'd turned that into a problem.

Another problem I associated with guide dogs, and one potentially less insulting to people over forty, was speed. Whenever I'd seen somebody with one they seemed to be walking very slowly and that wasn't for me at all. I walk really fast and am always in a rush, so, once again, I'd talked myself into believing that a guide dog and I wouldn't be compatible. As I said earlier, I viewed them as a hindrance and although I'd now agreed to apply for one, this opinion hadn't changed. I can be quite pig-headed sometimes and the fact that I'd got as far as agreeing to get one was amazing. Funnily enough, it was pointed out to me at the time by one of my grandparents that by refusing to accept change and being stubborn I was acting like an old person!

One thing I hadn't done at any point during this process was think about the benefits of having a guide dog. In fact, until I actually applied for one and started researching the whole subject, I genuinely didn't think there were any. Not for me, at least.

Now, the more I thought about it, the more convinced I became that I was about to do the right thing. I even made a little list of things that I wouldn't miss if I was successful in getting a guide dog. It was all about appreciating the potential benefits I was just talking about. I won't list them all, but many of them were little things such as not bumping into hedges and parked cars (they hurt a lot more than hedges) or boarding a busy train and not having a nightmare trying to find my seat. That used to happen to me a lot and if I had a pound for every story I had, I'd be rich. There I'd be, squinting away – I must have looked a right berk sometimes and was always self-conscious about it – until I inevitably ended up having to ask somebody where my seat was. By the time I sat down, I was either very frustrated, very flustered or both.

Having a cane made no difference whatsoever in this situation. If anything, it was a barrier. Just as I used to associate guide dogs with older people, those I came into contact with in the big, wide world would often associate white canes with older people, too. As a consequence, I'd often be treated quite strangely. I obviously couldn't see very clearly how people were looking at me but if I was using a cane, they'd either move out of the way so overtly as to make me believe it was in danger of knocking them over or speak to me like I was deaf. I found that both infuriating and demoralising and often came close to using the cane as a weapon.

What I understand now is that many people had the same preconceptions about those with canes as I did about those with guide dogs. Only perhaps they had more of an excuse – I, after all, was part of the club.

So I knew I wasn't going to miss using a cane: hitting people's ankles when I was out and about; misjudging their whereabouts on the pavement; being threatened with the police by an old lady whose leg I whacked in my hurry to catch a train . . . God, I hate canes. Did I mention that?

CHAPTER TWO

ENTER HATTI

As you may by now have gathered, after being attacked by that hedge the case for me getting a guide dog was unequivocal, and by the time I applied for one, I was actually quite excited. I think the biggest single argument for going ahead with it, at least as far as I was concerned, was putting my family's minds at rest and stopping them from worrying so much. Regardless of the fact that some of their fears might have been slightly exaggerated (I think they had visions of me walking off bridges and into rivers), the reality was that they had all become preoccupied with my wellbeing and that wasn't fair. The thing that worried *me* more than anything was being on my own outside in the dark. That incident with the hedge had alerted me to the fact that I didn't feel safe in that situation and I think a lot of other women probably feel the same, even without bad eyesight. As I said earlier, confidence had become a sixth sense for me and that was the only situation where it was absent. Also, if you're outwardly confident, people are far less likely to approach you, or so I'd heard.

My nearest branch of the charity Guide Dogs was in Leamington Spa and the first thing they did after me contacting them was to put me in touch with what's called a mobility team, local to my area. The team assesses applicants for things like their level of vision and how fast they walk. One of the first questions they asked me was whether I knew how to use a white cane. 'Yes,' I said suspiciously. 'Why do you need to know that?' They explained that in case the dog couldn't work for any reason, I'd need something to fall back on. I don't even know what I was expecting them to say, but even the mention of a white cane still gave me the creeps.

I'd been told by a few people that the assessment would be pretty stringent but, to be honest, it was nothing compared to some of the things I'd been through with the Paralympics. Some of the questions were quite personal, I suppose, but it takes a lot more than that to embarrass me. I'm quite an open person anyway and stuff like that just doesn't bother me.

They started by asking me how patient and tolerant I am. Short of moving in with you for a few months, that's not something they can test you for, so you have to be as honest with them as possible. And it's important. I'll give you an example as to why. Before my partner, Dan, who has even less vision than me, got his guide dog, Elmo (I'll introduce you to him later – Elmo is as mad as a lorryload of monkeys), Dan used Hatti once or twice when he came along with me while I was working and because he's quite impatient, it didn't work. Although she's a quick walker, Hatti likes to have a little bit of a sniff every now and then and she certainly doesn't like to be rushed. Some dogs need to be coaxed into working which you might think would make them unsuitable guide-dog material. Not so – because some people enjoy doing the coaxing. Also, if you're forever telling a dog that it's doing something wrong, it'll not only affect its confidence, but also its ability to do the job it's supposed to be doing. All of which just reinforces the idea that the more honest you are about your character and personality, the better your chance of getting the right dog.

Some people who have guide dogs have confidence issues which can prevent them from socialising, as a result of which their dog will be their entire world. I've spoken to people in this situation and although it might seem sad that somebody has difficulty finding friends and socialising, a guide dog can make life bearable for them. In some cases, it can also inspire them to take the first steps out of isolation, if you like. Stories like these are particularly heartening and they're also not that rare. I once met a blind lady at a guide-dog event who had recently had to give up her old dog after it became ill. She desperately wanted to keep it as they loved each other to pieces and had been through so much together, but because she lived in a small house, there wasn't enough room for her, the old dog and a new one, which she'd need in order to remain independent. I'd never seen anybody in that situation before and I don't mind admitting that it had a profound effect on me. She and the dog were considered to be inseparable, yet they were having to be separated. Practically, it made sense, but emotionally it was devastating. I definitely shed a tear or two that day.

Not long after that I heard a story about a guide dog in a family home. Their house caught fire one evening and the guide dog had gone upstairs and woken them all up. The two parents, one of whom was blind, managed to get each other downstairs and as they were doing that, the guide dog rounded the children up and did the same with them. I actually got to meet that dog at an awards ceremony a while ago and it was lovely. It's a German Shepherd and very friendly.

Anyway, the next question the mobility team asked me was what kind of journeys I'd be using the dog for. Again, this is all to do with temperament and situation. So, if a dog prefers the familiarity of going on the same journey, they might be best suited to somebody who isn't very active or who only visits the same few places. Some dogs also have quite short attention spans, so the longer the journey, the more likely you'll get lost. German Shepherds, for instance, prefer sticking to the same routes, or so I've heard, so if you have a predictable daily routine, they could be the dogs for you. I found this part so interesting, and it also made the prospect of getting a dog seem more real.

Unfortunately, they weren't allowed to take my word for it when I said I could use a cane and I had to go out and prove it to them. I managed to behave myself though, and as far as I know, I didn't injure anybody. Measuring my walking speed was the funniest thing. I treated it almost like a race, and when they asked me to begin, I went off like the wind. I forgot I was an athlete!

They broke it down into four speeds: slow, medium, fast and very fast. It took them a few attempts, but after having a chat with me they eventually put me in fast. The original idea was to put me in the very-fast bracket, but I had visions of being pulled around the country by a mad dog and not being able to stop. Perhaps having to slow down a bit wouldn't be such a bad thing.

After this, somebody else got in touch with me about whether or not I might need any other services – which I didn't; then someone called Adel contacted me and asked lots of questions about what I'd like to get out of having a guide dog, besides just getting from A to B. She also asked me a raft of questions about things like allergies and if I'd prefer a short- or long-haired dog. You can also express a preference for the sex of your dog, and even the colour. It sounds inane, I suppose, but some people find black dogs easier to see than yellow ones, and vice versa. It's that simple. Take Hatti, for instance. I wouldn't change her for the universe, yet I'm forever tripping over her. She seems to blend into the background quite well sometimes and, unfortunately, I often take a tumble.

Sometimes people's choice will be based on the kind of dog they've had previously. For instance, somebody might have had a black Labrador cross which was perfect for them and they won't want to deviate from that, which makes perfect sense.

As well as having no allergies, I had no real preference with regard to colour, sex or short-haired versus long-haired. I was also conscious of not being too prescriptive, given that there was up to a two-year wait.

What I did want, however, was a dog that was ok with children – dogs are like humans in this respect; some like kids and others don't – as in addition to hoping to start a family one day, I spent a lot of time going into schools to give talks. Another consideration had to do with loud noises. As an athlete, I'm either at the track, where there are starting guns going off all the time, or at the gym, where there's always lots of banging. A dog that's sensitive to loud noises wouldn't last very long at all with me, so that was essential.

Another question concerned where your dog goes to the toilet. They call it 'spending' in the guide-dog world (as in, spending a penny), and the reason they ask this is because the dog's preferences and yours need to match. Some dogs, for instance, only like going to the toilet on grass, which, if it's a number two, can be quite difficult to see and pick up sometimes. Some people prefer their dogs to go on concrete or hard surfaces which can, in turn, cause problems at home if they have a garden or a big lawn. What a minefield!

Having said this, unlike regular dog owners, people with guide dogs aren't obliged to clean up after their dogs. Some people can't, of course, but I think most who can do. I wouldn't dream of leaving a number two on the ground, for the simple reason that if I stood in one myself, I'd be furious.

I once tried explaining the whole vetting procedure to a friend of mine and he claimed that you get asked far fewer and less personal questions on a dating website. I've never been on one myself, but if one of the questions was, 'Where do you prefer going for a poo – on concrete or on a lawn?' I think I'd give up and go and live in a cave or something.

Once the whole thing was over, I was told by my contact at Guide Dogs that they'd be in touch once there was a match. As much as I wanted to ditch the white cane, I knew I had to manage my expectations with this. I'd spoken to somebody who'd allowed themselves to get a bit too excited about the prospect of getting a guide dog and their wait had been just under two years. I didn't want to put myself through that, so as much as I might have wanted to ring up the Guide Dogs people every other day and say, 'Have you found me one yet?' I managed to resist. Instead, I just carried on carrying on.

After three months, I had all but forgotten about getting a guide dog when one day, right out of the blue, the telephone rang.

'Is that Libby?' asked the person on the other end.

'Yes,' I said warily. I thought it was a nuisance call at first.

'It's Debbie at Guide Dogs here. How are you?'

Because the notion of me getting a guide dog had been put into storage at the back of my mind, it took me a moment or two to click as to why they might be calling. When it did, my stomach leaped and I went from being wary to quite excited.

'I'm fine, thank you,' I said excitedly. 'Have you found me a match?'

That last bit wasn't supposed to come out.

'Yes, I think we might have,' said Debbie, laughing. 'Would you like to hear about her?'

The answer to that was, of course, yes and for the next few minutes or so I listened very intently. The dog in question was a two-year-old black female Labrador cross and another person had tried her out but she walked too fast for them. So fortunately for me, the dog was available. I was then asked if I'd like to meet the dog, at which point my insides started doing somersaults. I'd done such a good job of forgetting about it that it all seemed very real now.

Still, I wasn't taking any chances, and I'm not sure Debbie would have had time to change her mind in the time it took me to answer.

'Yes, I'd love to meet her,' I said immediately. 'Can we arrange a time and a place?'

'That's actually the question I'm supposed to ask you,' said Debbie.

'Sorry!' I replied. 'I suppose I'm getting a little excited.'

'You're not the first one to do that,' said Debbie kindly.

I could tell that she'd probably had this conversation a hundred times before and when I put down the receiver having arranged a time, date and venue, I immediately called my parents to tell them the good news. The only thing I'd forgotten to ask Debbie was the dog's name, and instead of just ringing her back and asking, which I'm sure would have been fine, I spent two weeks wondering what it might be. All kinds of names went through my head and it became something of an obsession. Another one!

When the day finally came to meet my potential new guide dog, and hopefully, my new friend, I was in a right state. Not because of the name. I'd quite enjoyed wondering what it might be. I just didn't know what to expect. Up to now, she'd been living with her trainer who was going to be bringing her today.

During the hours leading up to her arrival I had some serious butterflies in my stomach and when the car pulled up outside my flat, they immediately turned into bats. Big ones! One of the first things people ask me when I'm being interviewed about having a guide dog is whether or not I come from a doggy family and the answer to that is, yes, I do. For as long as I can remember we always had dogs when I was a kid (Jack Russells, mainly). But not only were they not working dogs, they were also family dogs and despite the fact that I'd enjoyed playing with them and taking them for walks, the dogs at home were never my responsibility. The dog that had just arrived outside my house was a working dog, and, if we got on well together, would potentially become my guide dog and so my responsibility. It was all becoming very daunting and very real.

The other worry I had was what the dog in question, whose name I still didn't know, would think of me. That concern and potential dilemma had been fluttering around my consciousness more than any other in the two weeks since the phone call and I'd allowed it to keep me awake at night.

Incidentally, the only other thing that had been worrying

me about the meeting was the fact that it was all going to be observed by the dog's trainer. For some reason, I found that aspect slightly disconcerting, although it was obviously crucial. Humans can be strange sometimes, don't you think?

Anyway, I rushed to the front door and opened it. I was desperate to run over and say hello but nerves got the better of me, so I just stood there like a lemon. The trainer's name was Debbie – Hatti's puppy trainer – and when she got out of the car and saw me she waved. My central vision's virtually non-existent (it's actually a very pretty pattern, the kind you'd see in a kaleidoscope) but out of the corner of my left eye, I could just make out that there were two black dogs in the back of the car instead of one.

'Which one is she?' I asked Debbie after saying hello. 'And I don't even know her name yet.'

'Didn't they tell you? Her name's Hatti. She's the slightly smaller one. The other one's called Oxford. He's just along for the ride.'

When Debbie let the dogs out of the car, I think I was expecting Hatti to run into my arms or something. The scenario had popped into my head and I'd turned that into a prerequisite. In fact, she let me stroke her a bit but wasn't that interested. Oxford, on the other hand, was all over me like a rash. He also had a very real and dangerous wind problem. Even outside, it was absolutely horrendous, so it's not surprising that Hatti wasn't feeling sociable. It's a wonder she wasn't sick. I certainly would have been after being locked in a car with Oxford for more than five minutes.

'Don't worry,' said Debbie, sensing my disappointment. 'Guide dogs meet an awful lot of people. It's nothing personal. And apologies about Oxford. He's a very sweet-natured dog, bless him, but not quite as sweet-smelling.'

You're telling me!

I found out much later that although Hatti could be quite aloof with people sometimes, she also had an amazing memory. We didn't see Debbie for over three years after she eventually finished training Hatti and I, but when she pulled up outside my house one day, Hatti recognised the car and went absolutely bonkers. She hadn't even lived with Debbie for very long.

Going back to that first meeting though, Debbie was right: we always look at it from our point of view and not the dog's. Hatti had no idea that she was coming to meet somebody she might be living and working with. I was just yet another human being who, unless they had something interesting to play with, or, better still, something tasty to eat, wasn't worth bothering with. Fortunately, I'd thought ahead on this front and, after asking Debbie's permission, I fetched a bag of dog treats and set about trying to make myself popular. I didn't have the heart not to give Oxford any, despite knowing full well what the result would be.

The treats definitely had the desired effect, and I went from being, in movie terms, a lowly extra to a decent supporting actress with a line or two in a matter of seconds. Now interested in what I might have hidden elsewhere, Hatti led the way through my front door and into my living room. I took this to be a good sign, despite the fact that Hatti was clearly just interested in what I might have in my kitchen. Small steps and all that.

After having a sniff around the living room and then the kitchen (Oxford had been put back in the car by this point) Hatti made her way out into the garden, where, would you believe it, somebody had planted a few new doggie toys. I wonder who could have done that? These didn't go down anywhere near as well as the treats, but you have to be thankful for small mercies, I suppose, and after a little bit of gentle coaxing, she did me a favour and fetched a ball once or twice. In fact, I think it would have worked better the other way around to be honest, with Hatti throwing something for me! It genuinely did seem as if she was humouring me. In some ways she seemed to think and act more like a human than a dog. It was fascinating.

Once the 'getting-to-know-you' bit was over, Debbie surprised me with a question. 'Would you like to take Hatti out for a walk?' she asked.

'What, you mean with a harness on? Like in proper guide-dog mode?'

'Yes,' she said smiling, 'with a harness on. But Hatti won't be guiding you – you'll be guiding her. Just a short walk. You obviously like each other, so why not?'

Oh my God! I hadn't expected this. Although I'd spoken to plenty of people with guide dogs in the past, I didn't actually know one as a friend, nor had I even met a guide dog before, let alone taken one out for a walk. After pausing for a few seconds,

I said yes, and while I carried on stroking Hatti, Debbie went off to the car to fetch a harness.

After showing me how to put the harness on, Debbie told me to get a route sorted in my head that I was comfortable with and that wasn't too complicated. Once I'd done that, we were good to go.

Believe it or not, the first emotion I felt after putting the harness on Hatti was embarrassment. It sounds awful, doesn't it? It was totally unexpected, but for some reason, standing there with a guide dog in front of me, holding on to a harness, had exactly the same effect as the cane.

'Where are you going?' asked Debbie.

'Just to the local supermarket,' I replied. 'It's only about five or ten minutes away. I need to buy a couple of things, so we should be about half an hour. Will that be ok?'

I was getting braver now.

'Absolutely,' said Debbie. 'It'll be perfect practice.'

Before we left, Debbie taught me one or two instructions that I might need to use and after going through those in my head one final time we were ready for the off.

I have to admit that the first few yards were horrible, as the moment we hit the pavement, the embarrassment and self-consciousness multiplied tenfold. There were lots of cars passing us, and even though I couldn't see the drivers or passengers, it felt like they were staring at us. Paranoid? Me? The thing that changed this was the feeling I was getting from Hatti through the harness. Unlike me, she seemed to be confident as well as comfortable, and while quelling my feelings of embarrassment and self-consciousness, this also began to set me at ease.

When we got to the first road, which was just a backstreet, really, Hatti reached the kerb and then stopped. Guide dogs are trained to sit down when they reach the side of a road, but Hatti's never been good at that. She much prefers to stand. Just then, an approaching car started to slow down, and although there was no actual crossing there, it stopped just before us. I couldn't believe it. If I'd had a cane, it would have flown past, but because I had a guide dog with me, it actually stopped. In the end, I had to wave them past with a 'thank you', as Debbie had told me that guide dogs are trained to wait until a car has passed in case there's also traffic coming the other way.

From then on, things just got better and better and by the time we got to the supermarket, I'd reached the conclusion that the difference between the reaction I got with a cane and the one I got with a guide dog came down to two things: awareness and courtesy. As soon as people see a guide dog, they become super aware and nine times out of ten, they'll either stop, slow down or move out of the way. It was a revelation, and as we walked into the supermarket, I remember asking myself why I hadn't done this earlier.

Inside, things had a slightly different feel, because as well as there being no cars in the vicinity, we were also in much closer proximity to other people. We were also around food, and I had no idea what people's reaction would be to a dog being present. Fortunately, everybody seemed to be quite comfortable with having a – as I'd later find out – permanently hungry food thief in their midst and the courtesy that was shown to me continued.

Debbie had told me just before we left that if I needed any help in the supermarket, I should just go up to the information desk and ask. 'They're usually very helpful,' she said. Although I didn't say so to Debbie, I'd had one or two experiences that taught me otherwise when using a cane, so I was a little sceptical about her optimism. Even so, I thought I'd give it a whirl, and after thinking of something I might need that was right at the other end of the supermarket, I decided to pretend I didn't know where I was going and see what happened.

'Excuse me,' I said approaching the desk. 'Would somebody be able to take me to the bread section, please?'

Two people were sitting behind the desk and as soon as they saw Hatti, one of them stood up. 'I'll take you with pleasure,' she said. 'Follow me, would you?'

I couldn't believe it!

From the moment we left the information desk to the moment we arrived at the bread section, the woman who was guiding us chatted away like an old friend. She couldn't have been nicer or more helpful.

The thing that amazed me the most about Hatti on that first walk was how intelligent and confident she was. It felt like she was teaching me, which I suppose she was in a way. And I was more than happy to learn. I'd been using the commands that Debbie had taught me before the walk, but Hatti had been doing them automatically, so while I was supposed to be taking *her* for a walk, she was definitely in charge. The only thing I had to do was tell Hatti if we were going left or right as she obviously didn't know the way. She did the rest. I just couldn't get my head around the fact that dogs can learn left from right and to watch one actually doing it, and so effortlessly, was staggering.

The most beneficial thing from that first walk, apart from Hatti preventing me from being run over and enabling me to receive friendly treatment at the information desk, was her taking me around certain objects that were in the way, including human beings. With or without a cane, under normal circumstances I'd be bumping into objects and people all the time, whereas Hatti just whizzed me around all of them. My absolute nemesis when trying to negotiate my way around the pavements of Great Britain was always telephone exchange boxes. You know, those green things, about three or four feet high. This is partly because of where they're positioned, which is usually on the very inside of a pavement, almost hidden away, and partly because they often seem to blend into their surroundings. From the day I left school until the day I got Hatti, hardly a day went by without me clattering into one, and the language that used to follow could only be described as industrial.

There were two telephone exchange boxes on the way to the supermarket and even though I'd long since learned to avoid them, the fact that Hatti did this automatically had me grinning from ear to ear like a Cheshire cat. She was like Superdog!

Actually, I did have one other nemesis and that was litter bins. I often used to mistake these for children when I used a cane and spent half my young life apologising to them. Litter bins, that is. After a few seconds, I'd usually work out what had happened and feel myself going crimson. The realisation that I'd been talking to a litter bin in broad daylight and on a busy pavement used to mortify me.

When I got back to my flat Debbie was very keen to find out how it had gone and I was only too keen to tell her. 'That was just amazing,' I began. 'In fact,' I said, patting Hatti probably just a little bit too enthusiastically, '*she's* amazing!' Debbie didn't seem at all surprised by my reaction and after showing me how to remove the harness, she made a suggestion that she said should cement the relationship. 'I think a treat might be in order,' said Debbie. 'Don't you?'

Had it been up to me, Hatti wouldn't have gone home with Debbie that afternoon. She'd have stayed with me on the sofa eating treats while I told her how amazing she was. As nice as that would have been, it would probably have turned Hatti's head, so it was better that we followed protocol. What a day though!

CHAPTER THREE

GETTING TO KNOW YOU

The following morning, Debbie called me with her verdict on how she thought the visit had gone. She'd told me before leaving that she'd let me know her decision as soon as possible and it had taken all of my resolve not to try and pin her down to a time. She kicked off the conversation with a question. 'I'll tell you what, Libby,' she said. 'How do *you* think it went yesterday?'

'I thought it went brilliantly,' I said, having decided not to hold back. 'Once you told me that Hatti wasn't being aloof with me I started to relax a little and as you know, the walk went really well.'

'Ok,' said Debbie. 'I just wanted to make sure you hadn't changed your mind. It happens sometimes.'

'You mean—'

'Yes,' said Debbie, continuing my sentence for me. 'Hatti and you are obviously a good match, so in a couple of weeks she'll be coming to live with you, if that's ok?'

'That's more than ok,' I said. 'Thank you!'

My emotions were a complete jumble when I put down the phone. I was thrilled that Hatti would be coming to live with me, but until it was all confirmed the only parts I'd properly considered were the ones that I could imagine, i.e. Hatti helping me get from A to B and the two of us having some fun together. The moment I put the phone down, every single other scenario came rushing into my head. What if she was ill? Which vet would I take her to? Where would she sleep? What if I had to go away and she couldn't come with me? What if she hated living here? What about my landlord? The vast majority of these scenarios had either already been discussed with Debbie or were easily solved with either a simple telephone call or a 'rational' thought process.

One of my biggest fears after receiving Debbie's telephone call (and this one was not unfounded) was how Hatti would cope with life at the track. Anyway, that was for later. In the meantime, I had just two weeks to get both myself and my flat in order for Hatti's arrival.

The first thing I did once I'd pulled myself together was to go out and buy the most expensive dog bed I could find. Now that I'm a mother I can compare this to what it's like when you're expecting a baby, but in many ways this was worse, as instead of having a partner and a busload of overexcited grandparents and friends ready to help me spend ridiculous amounts of money on ridiculously flash pushchairs, I was on my own. And me on my own in this situation meant there was nobody there to rein me in – to remind me that I might be on the verge of bankrupting myself, or to point out that the bed I was about to buy had a non-detachable cover, which meant it was almost impossible to wash properly and no amount of hoovering or Febreze would counter that.

Buy of the century, it was not.

In addition to the world's most impractical dog bed, I also bought Hatti two shiny new bowls, and come the day of her arrival, I was actually slightly less nervous than I had been prior to and during our first meeting. Although we'd only been on one short walk, I already had complete confidence in Hatti and the overriding emotions I experienced prior to her arrival were excitement and anticipation. Excitement because she was coming to live with me and I couldn't wait to get to know her, and anticipation because I knew that we'd be going on lots of new adventures together. It was all good.

Nevertheless, I deliberately kept Hatti's arrival low key and instead of making a great big fuss of her when she arrived, I acted as though she was already in residence. This seemed to work well and one of the first things Hatti did when Debbie left, apart from sniffing out the kitchen, of course, was to start playing with her toys. I was surprised at how playful she was and right from the get-go, she seemed very happy. We spent our first evening together snuggled up on the sofa watching rubbish TV and when Hatti was ready to call it a night, she took herself off, grabbed one of her toys and went to bed. I was conscious not to crowd or bother Hatti when she moved in, so whenever she went to her bed, regardless of what time of day it was, I'd always leave her to it. As it turns out, Hatti loves having her own space occasionally, so this was important.

The following week was all about the two of us getting to know one another and about Hatti acclimatising to her new surroundings. For the first few days, I watched her like a hawk with some peripheral vision. Not because I was expecting her to do anything bad (she was fully house trained and hadn't been known to chew furniture), but because I wanted her to be happy and if she wasn't, I wanted to know straight away.

The only thing I noticed behaviour-wise in that first week or so was that while we were in the house Hatti didn't like letting me out of her sight (so that was mutual). This, according to Debbie, was perfectly natural. My confidence in Hatti's confidence, so to speak, was slightly exaggerated and it was all part of her settling in. On day three, I went for a bath sometime in the afternoon and left the bathroom door open. After washing my hair, I ducked my head under the water to rinse it and as I came back up again, there was Hatti leaning right over the side of the bath and staring at me. It was like something out of a horror movie! My initial reaction was to duck back under and I ended up banging the back of my head. I almost drowned.

The next time I had a bath, instead of creeping in while I had my head under water and then scaring the living daylights out of me, Hatti strolled in shortly after I got in and just curled up on the bath mat. It was quite nice, to be honest, and her being a bit clingy made me feel like *I* could do something for *her*, as opposed to it being the other way around.

What surprised me the most about that first week was how active Hatti could be in the garden. She'd seemed very measured during our first meeting and I'd had the feeling that even when she felt comfortable there wouldn't be that much more going on. How wrong was I? On about day three Hatti went from being a fairly playful, but nevertheless slightly guarded off-duty guide dog, to a complete flaming nutcase! I couldn't believe it. As somebody who is active for a living and has trouble sitting still, this suited me down to the ground and we spent literally hours together playing games and messing around. It was such a nice surprise and, more than anything else, is probably what bonded us together.

The following week Hatti and I started a two-week training course which is obligatory for all new guide-dog owners. Hatti had already been on this course with her previous owner but didn't seem to mind doing it again. As I said earlier, it always felt like she was training me in those early days and I think that also helped us to bond.

On the first day of the course, they taught me how to ensure that Hatti was fit and healthy. This meant checking her mouth, her eyes and her ears, but especially her paws. Because working dogs can spend a lot time on their feet, they're prone to getting thorns and other bits stuck in their paws, so making sure they're free of things like that is essential.

After that, it was on to grooming. For some reason, I didn't feel very comfortable about grooming Hatti prior to this, so being taught how to do it properly, and that it's actually ok, was really helpful. They also showed me how to pick her up properly, which was helpful and would come in useful if I ever had to take Hatti to the vet, for example. As it turned out, the first time I had to lift Hatti was down to a phobia, rather than illness, but I'll come to that later.

Next up was how to give Hatti medication, which, like grooming, I didn't feel too comfortable with going into the course. I had a feeling that when it came to taking tablets or other medicines, dogs would be like children and it would be tricky. I was right. I didn't have to actually give Hatti a tablet during the instruction, but they taught me how to prise open her mouth and make her swallow. I didn't enjoy this very much and neither did Hatti, but it was a key part of the course and, over the years, I've had to follow these instructions several times. Hatti absolutely hates having to take tablets and had I not received this training, we'd probably have ended up wrestling on the floor on more than one occasion; but although she always puts up a bit of a fight, she always comes around in the end.

After covering all of the above, we moved on to Hatti and I working together, and the majority of this training took place at, or at least started from, my house. Debbie had trained Hatti, so it made sense for her to train me *and* Hatti. After turning up at the house one morning, she set about expanding on what she'd taught me on that first day. According to Debbie, the best way for me to learn was 'on the job', so to speak, and we started off by getting Hatti used to some of my most frequently travelled routes. The most obvious one was from my house to the track – a journey I did up to seven days a week – and while it was almost second nature to me, with Hatti it would be like starting again. Suddenly, that walk to the supermarket almost a month earlier seemed like a very distant memory and when I put on Hatti's harness in readiness to set off, I was once again attacked by a swarm of butterflies. The journey to the supermarket had been little more than a short walk and I'd only had to ask Hatti to go left or right. This time she'd require more input from me. The question was, would I be able to deliver? Fortunately, Debbie came with us that first time (it was like having stabilisers on) and generally we got on ok. Because I knew the route to the track so well, all I had to do was to say the correct commands at the correct time (easier said than done if you've got butterflies!), and once again, Hatti was coolness personified. We really did seem to click when it came to getting from A to B and I was certain that if there'd been a competition for the best guide dog and owner, we'd have been up there.

This flush of success must have caught Debbie's attention, as the following day, she had a surprise for us. 'Today we're going to do variables,' she said with a smile.

'What, you mean some different routes?'

'Not exactly,' she said. 'I'm talking more about roadworks and pavements that have cars parked on them. That sort of thing.'

Blast! Everything had gone so smoothly so far and I hadn't even considered things like roadworks.

Debbie explained that although guide dogs are usually fine going around litter bins and the like, things like barriers and roadworks can be confusing, especially on a route that a dog is particularly used to. We also covered situations like cars pulling out of driveways. This wasn't exactly out of the ordinary, but it could happen anywhere, and it was important that we were ready for it. Also, Debbie mentioned the fact that guide dogs can sometimes forget things and because Hatti hadn't worked in a while, it was important to give her a refresher.

When it came to cars pulling out of driveways, Hatti was absolutely on the nail, but Debbie still advised me to test her. Not just on this, but in other situations, too. Hatti wasn't flustered or confused by the roadworks we came across; these were on a specific route prepared to test her and she coped brilliantly.

My admiration for Hatti's ability was tempered slightly by something Debbie said during training one day. She certainly wasn't trying to belittle Hatti's capabilities, but when talking about how aware you should be when walking with a guide dog, she said it was best to err on the side of caution and think of them as toddlers. At first, I thought she was making a joke of some kind, but she wasn't. 'If a toddler was leading you on a walk,' she said, 'you'd always make sure you had a tight hold of their hand just in case something happened. It's the same with a guide dog. They're not infallible by any means, so are not exempt from losing concentration, making mistakes or doing things unexpectedly. They can also be very temperamental, so you have to be on your guard at all times, for both your sakes.'

I have to admit that this was a reality check for me as in my mind Hatti was already Superdog and should have been wearing at least a cape. If anything though, it made me care about Hatti even more and made me think of our relationship on the road as more of a partnership, which is what it is anyway.

When explaining the above, Debbie also mentioned kryptonite. 'A lot of guide dogs have kryptonite,' she said. 'And with Hatti it's set off by squirrels.'

What Debbie was referring to was basically a situation or object that makes a guide dog go a bit loopy or stop working for a while. I'd always assumed they were unflappable but, at the end of the day, it doesn't matter how much training they receive or what environment they live in – dogs are dogs.

Once again, I think this helped me to bond a little bit better with Hatti as it made her seem less like a machine, which is almost how I saw guide dogs prior to meeting her, and more like a regular dog. Now I knew what Hatti's kryptonite was I couldn't wait for us to see a squirrel. According to Debbie, she would just trot towards the squirrel and want to play with it, as opposed to wanting to rip it to pieces, so I wasn't too worried that I'd be dragged across a busy road or halfway up a tree. Apparently, pigeons have the same effect on some guide dogs, but I'm not sure I could handle that. Imagine being in a town centre? It'd be a nightmare. Where I live, in Loughborough, they're absolutely everywhere, so it'd take me hours to get from A to B.

Guide-dog kryptonite was an entertaining concept, but I'm sure it could become quite draining. Fortunately, all the areas I've lived in since getting together with Hatti haven't been too squirrel-heavy. The first time Hatti and I encountered one together we were on our way to the track. The reason I knew there was a squirrel in our midst was because she suddenly stopped dead without any warning and then started pulling me to the right in the direction of a large tree. She was also quite excited which was at odds with her usual demeanour when working. Within a few seconds, the squirrel had made its escape and we were on our way again but I was glad it had happened. It was an enjoyable interlude and, to be honest, it probably pulled me out of autopilot and back into the here and now, which was where I was supposed to be.

Something I haven't mentioned yet is what guide dogs get up to when they're off duty. Taking a guide dog for a regular walk and letting them go mad is part of the training. You're supposed to take your guide dog for at least one big off-duty walk a week, but Hatti usually needs two or three (one long and a couple of shorter ones) and I'll play it by ear as to when we go – a day when we haven't done much is the ideal time. It's so important to let them behave like normal dogs and there's nothing I love more than watching and hearing Hatti go a bit mad.

Another thing we covered during training was what to do when another dog pays your guide too much attention, if you see what I mean, or if they're attacked. Unfortunately, the latter happened during one of our training sessions with Debbie and it was horrifying. We were on our way back from the track and were walking through a park when, all of a sudden, a Terrier attacked Hatti. What you're supposed to do in that situation is let go of the harness and the lead, so the dog can make its escape if it wants to – and that's exactly what I did. Poor Hatti was absolutely terrified, bless her. The Terrier had nipped her quite badly and although it hadn't drawn blood, she had several marks on her leg. What made it worse was that the dog's owner wasn't at all bothered and seemed to think that because it hadn't drawn blood there was no problem. I was quite taken aback, but Debbie wasn't, and after the owner had expressed her indifference to the incident Debbie tore a strip off her. If you see a working dog, you're supposed to keep your dog on a lead, she explained. It's common sense – especially if your dog can be feisty, which this one certainly was. The woman tried defending herself, but she was fighting a losing battle; in the end, she just shuffled off looking slightly daft. She didn't even apologise, for heaven's sake. After making sure Hatti was ok, we all went on our way, but poor Hatti wasn't herself for the rest of the day. Come to think of it, neither was I.

There was a really bad case in Leicester a few years ago where a Staffordshire cross attacked a guide dog in the city centre. Apparently, the Staffy went straight for the guide dog's throat, resulting in hours and hours of surgery. The guide dog went back to work but was terrified of everything and had to be retired a few months later. The owner of the Staffy was prosecuted and sadly, because of poor ownership, the dog was put to sleep, so it ended badly for all parties. Had the dog been on a lead, as it probably should have been in a city centre on a busy day, it would not have happened.

I'm pleased to report that nothing like this has happened to Hatti since that day, although I do get people coming up to me sometimes and telling me how and why their dogs hate guide dogs. 'My dog's a right miserable so-and-so,' a man once said to me. 'He can't stand guide dogs.' Fair enough. At the end of the day though, a dog getting spooked by another dog wearing a luminous yellow harness is no different from Hatti getting excited by a squirrel, which is why it's best to get them on a lead when you see one.

One of the most interesting parts of the training was how to take public transport and it's gifted me a plethora of stories. Hatti is a lot smaller than most other passengers and despite having a coloured harness on, she can often go unseen. So, what I always try to do, regardless of whether we're on a bus or a train, is to give her as much space as possible – because as well as allowing her to feel comfortable, our fellow travellers are more likely to see her, and, most importantly, not tread on her.

The only thing that really spooks Hatti when we're travelling, which is another reason why I always try and create space for her, is people who throw their bags down on the ground. I totally get why they do this, but unfortunately, it scares Hatti half to death and there's little I can do about it.

Going back to what Debbie suggested earlier – that people are always nice when you have a guide dog – when I was heavily pregnant with my son, Edward, Hatti and I had to take a train one day, but when we got in the carriage every seat was taken. It wouldn't normally have bothered me, but my feet were absolutely killing me at the time and I wasn't feeling too steady. Nobody offered their seat though, so I just had to resign myself to standing. I was literally waddling, by the way, and had a bump the size of a beach ball. Another passenger who was also standing kept asking me if I was ok and the longer this went on, the more irate he became. He wanted to say something on my behalf, but I asked him not to. If the passengers sitting down weren't prepared to offer me a seat off their own bats, they weren't worth bothering with. Happily, this has only happened on a couple of occasions – the vast majority of people couldn't be more helpful.

My partner, Dan, isn't quite as 'British' as I am when it comes to saying nothing and if he'd been in the carriage with us, there'd have been blood. He's experienced a lot more problems than I have in this department and, for some reason, it always seems to end in an argument. To be fair, he's had people telling him that guide dogs shouldn't be allowed on trains which is why he practises a zero-tolerance policy.

Travelling on trains was actually one of the most beneficial parts of the training as I had a boyfriend living in Edinburgh at the time and was going up there every other weekend. I discovered which carriages were the best for Hatti and me to travel in, as some of them had seats with slightly more legroom. The training also gave me practice in negotiating different platforms and where to go for help. And if I couldn't find anyone else to ask, I'd go to the front of the train and ask the driver, which used to surprise them a bit.

*

During the training period, I wasn't allowed to take Hatti out without Debbie, other than for a normal walk, which we did at the local field. Before Hatti and I could work together, I had to be carefully assessed and fortunately, although it was quite a long and rigorous process, I passed without a hitch. I remember when we finished it. After a cup of tea, Debbie said, 'Right, I've got to go now.' We said our goodbyes and then she added, 'It's just you and Hatti from here on in. Are you excited?'

'Do you know,' I said, 'I think I am.'

'Cool,' said Debbie. 'Make sure you give us a shout if you have any problems.' And with that, she closed the front door behind her, got in her car and drove away.

Hatti and I had spent the previous three weeks together, but apart from playing in the garden and going for the odd walk, we'd always had Debbie in tow. Now Hatti joined me on the sofa and I gave her a stroke. Despite having taken exams in the past, this was the first time I'd ever been nervous about passing anything and when it started to sink in I felt really chuffed. Hatti and I were now a team.

CHAPTER FOUR

AWAY FROM HOME

Shortly before the 2014 Commonwealth Games started, BBC Scotland asked if they could send a reporter and cameraman to one of my training sessions. I was apparently one of Scotland's gold-medal hopes and it ended up being Hatti's first appearance on television. Without a single word of a lie, she was an absolute tart in front of the TV camera. I was asked by the reporter to rub Hatti's tummy for a couple of minutes, but instead of just lying there with her tongue lolling out like she normally did, she started rolling around in ecstasy. I think I actually called her a tart on camera, but fortunately, it was under my breath and the microphone didn't catch it.

It was about three months after Hatti and I became a team that I had to go and compete. I think I was away for about two weeks in all, and because Hatti hadn't been with me very long, I was nervous about who she would stay with. Unfortunately, I couldn't take her with me, so it was something I just had to accept. In the end, I settled on splitting the time between my mum and my dad. Mum and Dad had separated by then, and with both of them being doggy mad and knowing Hatti, it made perfect sense.

The only thing that worried me slightly was how Hatti would get on with Mum and Dad's dogs – and in particular my dad's. For some reason, his Jack Russell hates black dogs like Hatti, and although he'd never been nasty to her before, I was worried that Hatti being on his territory might change things. I've since learned that dogs disliking black dogs is quite common in Dogland, but I have no idea why.

Dad's dog was very aloof when she was there and went out of his way to avoid her, but he didn't take things any further and, according to Dad, Hatti learned to just keep out of his way. Seven years on and nothing's changed, really. Occasionally they see each other, and while Hatti will always extend an olive branch by going to say hello, he will literally huff, turn the other way and walk off. Typical male behaviour.

What I hadn't bargained for was the effect that Hatti moving in with them would have on my mum and dad. I only found out afterwards that the prospect of having a working dog to stay was actually quite daunting for them, just as it had been for me, I suppose, when I first got to know her.

I'd told Mum and Dad as much as I could beforehand, but there were always going to be things that I'd forgotten, and one of them was that when going for an off-duty walk Hatti was prone to being a little unpredictable. Just like me, Dad's preconception of guide dogs was that they did as they were told at all times and basically behaved like robots, so he was in for a bit of a shock.

When it came to letting Hatti off her lead during their first walk together everything went smoothly at first. I'd told Dad that after telling her to sit down he should take off her lead and then tell her she could go, but only when he was ready. Unfortunately, Dad didn't get as far as the last bit, as the moment he took off Hatti's lead, instead of waiting to be excused, she jumped straight into a nearby beck and started playing. In the end, Dad realised that Hatti was just a normal dog and, in human terms, this was her Saturday night out after a hard week. I think he ended up throwing stones into the beck for Hatti to retrieve but she didn't. (All she ever does in that situation is to run to where they've landed, look into the water and then look up again and wait for the next one.) I think my dad was hoping she'd catch one or two, but the fact is Hatti couldn't catch a cold, I'm afraid. I took her up to my Dad's just a few weeks ago and we played exactly the same game. She loves it.

When it came to staying at my mum's house, Hatti was made to feel more welcome, at least from the doggy side. Mum's dog, Rosie, who is a Heinz 57, absolutely adores Hatti and as well as hanging out together, they sleep in the same bed and even eat together. I think they originally bonded over fox poo, which is fairly typical, apparently.

When those two went out together you could tell that they had one thing on their minds and that was having fun. Rosie's a little bit older now and slightly less playful but they still have a great relationship, although Rosie's getting a little bit cantankerous and sometimes, instead of sharing a bed, they'll fight over it. Mum bought Rosie a new one a few months ago and because Rosie is tiny, the bed is tiny, too. To Hatti, this presented an opportunity to indulge in one of her favourite pastimes, which is fitting into small spaces. To be fair, she's actually very good at it and, over the years, has squeezed herself into places only a Chihuahua should be able to get into. Anyway, one day, when Hatti was staying with Mum, she decided to move in and squat in Rosie's tiny crate for a couple of hours. Mum was at her wits' end, thinking that Hatti had done a runner, but after searching for her for an hour or so, she eventually found her curled up in a tiny ball inside Rosie's crate.

Despite being born in England and to English parents, I competed for Scotland at the 2014 Commonwealth Games. I'd lived on the border of the country for such a long time, been educated there and also been supported throughout much of my career by Sport Scotland. It seemed right somehow.

Taking part in a major competition on home soil is always a very special experience, and after winning silver at the 2012 Paralympic Games in London, I was hoping to go one better. As soon as the Games commenced, Glasgow was sparkling, with an amazing and uplifting atmosphere. It was a very similar atmosphere to London 2012 – everyone was super friendly and the weather was just fabulous. The athletic events took place at the legendary Hampden Park Stadium and you could hear every one of the 51,000 people in the stands.

This sounds daft, but one of my favourite parts of competing at the Commonwealth Games was that the track they'd installed at Hampden Park was blue. I know, it's ridiculous isn't it? It makes absolutely no difference to how you perform – or at least it shouldn't – but as soon as I saw it, I thought, Ooh, a blue track – that looks nice! If I had to give you a reason for preferring to run on a blue track, I'd say it was probably because they're not very common. It's just a novelty, I suppose.

I ended up achieving my goal of improving on my performance in London by winning gold in the T12 100m. Athletes competing in the T12 class have a higher visual acuity than those in the T11 class. I knew that one day I'd end up competing in T11 because of the degenerative nature of my condition, but for the time being I was still in T12.

The only thing I didn't like about the Games was not having Hatti there. For the previous three months or so, we'd spent almost every waking hour together and it felt like I'd lost a limb or something. Sure, she helps me get around, but we'd become inseparable and that was as much by choice as anything else. When I went for a bath Hatti still came and sat on the mat and when she went out into the garden I'd usually end up following her. I'd like to be able to say that Hatti missed me as much as I missed her but if I did, I'd be lying. According to Mum and Dad she had a great time with them, and I think she was just happy to have a break. Also, having some doggy company must have been nice for her.

These days, if I have to go away, Hatti isn't herself, and she'll be quite clingy with whoever's looking after her. The thing is, it's exactly the same when Dan goes away with his dog, Elmo. All of a sudden, Hatti will become very clingy and won't leave my side. It's either because she feels vulnerable or because she feels responsible for me. Either way, it's incredibly sweet, although it can get awkward when I want to go to the loo!

When Hatti saw me for the first time after the Games she became quite animated. It was almost as if she'd forgotten about me for two weeks and had then remembered me again. Oh my God, it's you – I thought you'd died! Even so, tearing her away from my dad's clutches was easier said than done as she absolutely adores him. I call him the dog whisperer as all dogs just seem to gravitate towards him.

About a week after the Commonwealth Games had finished, I had to take Hatti on her first ever flight. To say I wasn't really looking forward to this would be a massive understatement for the simple reason that it was a trip into the unknown. After the hullabaloo of the Games, I'd been looking forward to some peace and quiet and the last thing I wanted was a new experience. I was also a bit of a nervous flyer, so having Hatti with me would potentially compound that.

Being partially sighted at an airport can be quite intimidating. For a start, there are usually hundreds of people rushing around, dragging luggage behind them and because they're often in a rush, simple things like courtesy and care go out of the window. That's to say nothing about reading the electronic screens or getting to the gates.

The flight itself was only to Scotland and would last about an hour. I'd been invited to a load of events up there after winning gold at the Games and despite not knowing how Hatti would handle the journey, I knew it would be so much quicker than taking the train. As with the task of getting from A to B without a cane, this would inevitably end in me either turning up at the wrong gate, getting pushed over or bumped a hundred times. Or, worst of all, having to ask somebody for help.

If you're flying with a guide dog, you have to ring up the airline first to tell them. What they do then is to add the dog to the booking, but instead of saying 'guide dog', it'll say something like, 'Passenger X'. Whether there's a reason for that I don't know, but in my experience, that's how airlines identify a guide dog. The dog always has a seat reserved next to you.

Instead of a special doggy seat belt, you're given an attachment that allows you to fix your own seat belt to the dog's lead. To be honest, they're probably not massively secure but it's the best you can do in that situation and it prevents the dog from running off.

When Hatti and I got to the airport, I quickly realised that guide dogs were not frequent flyers, but instead of us being treated like some kind of curiosity, we were treated like royalty. Hatti in particular received an incredible amount of fuss and it came from all quarters. The airport in question was East Midlands and because the majority of passengers were on their way to somewhere sunny, the atmosphere in the place was great. I expect it would be different if everyone was travelling on business, but on that particular day they weren't and we were happy to reap the benefits.

Despite my reluctance around asking for assistance, and the fact that back then I was as stubborn as I was proud, I knew I'd need some help on this occasion as I wasn't sure about airport protocol. As it turns out though, this just added to the experienceas the staff couldn't get enough of Hatti, or she of them.

The only part I was still nervous about after checking in was going through security but once again, everyone was brilliant. Sometimes people can be a little bit patronising when you have a guide dog and tend to smother you. I got none of that on this occasion and the people we encountered just seemed pleased to see us. Or should I say, pleased to see Hatti. I could have been anyone!

Fortunately, the flight wasn't very busy, so Hatti and I had a row to ourselves. I was still nervous at this point but Hatti seemed to be enjoying herself so once I was safely in my seat I began to relax. By now, and because I'd been a bit nervous, I must have given her at least two days' worth of treats but because it had all gone so smoothly I didn't mind at all. Then, a fellow passenger reached for some biscuits. Hatti heard him undoing the wrapper, lifted her head and stared in the man's direction. The biscuits were presumably a freebie from the airline as all of a sudden I could hear wrapper noises coming from all over the plane, and so could Hatti! She must have thought it was her birthday watching a man liberate some free biscuits but unfortunately she was out of luck. I appreciate she gets the odd titbit now and then but I would never knowingly allow Hatti to take food from a stranger as I have no idea what it is. As it was, she really couldn't have given a monkey's about being on an aeroplane or going on her first flight and just sat there staring at the man with the biscuits.

Speaking of food, on another occasion I bought myself a pot of yogurt and granola before the flight and this time, just before take-off I opened my pot of yogurt and granola and, as I did so, some honey flew into the air and landed on one of her front paws. Suddenly, she became perfectly content and she spent the entire flight – about an hour – removing the honey from her paw. She's got such a sweet tooth!

Going back to that first flight though, as far as my confidence was concerned, it did me the power of good, and although subsequent experiences at airports haven't always been as convivial (or, in Hatti's case, as abundant), I know what's what and who to ask if I ever get into trouble. Hatti and I know Birmingham, East Midlands, Manchester and Glasgow airports like the back or our hands and paws these days and flying's become a doddle. Also, because guide dogs are still a rarity on flights, people are still polite, so touch wood, Hatti and I have never had a bad experience so far. If you see us though, please don't feed her biscuits – I guarantee she'll already have had enough.

*

One of the events that Hatti and I went to when we were in Scotland was the Sports Personality of the Year Awards which Lewis Hamilton ended up winning. He was the only other sportsperson to bring a dog with them that night and because he's Lewis Hamilton, his dog took the majority of the limelight. I remember us standing on the red carpet when suddenly Lewis turned up with his bulldog. One minute Hatti was sporting dog personality of the year and the next she was runner-up! We didn't mind though. Just being at the same event as people like Lewis Hamilton was a real thrill and my only regret is that Hatti and I didn't bump into them both on the red carpet.

That aside, it was a bizarre evening for me. I'd been asked to present an award and make a speech and instead of doing it on my own, I was to do it with Eddie Izzard. I'd never met Eddie before, but the two of us got on great and we managed to get through it – just! We presented the BBC Get Inspired Unsung Hero Award to swimming coach Jill Stidever and once we'd left the stage, Jess Glynne and Clean Bandit came on and performed a couple of numbers.

One of my sponsors at the time was the energy company SSE, and they had a box at the event. Until being asked to speak with Eddie and present an award by the organisers I'd been due to stay in the box for the entire event, and, getting into Hatti mode, enjoy the hospitality on offer. I'd heard they were having my favourite food, mac and cheese, but unfortunately because of my commitment to presenting I was having to sit near the stage. Thankfully SSE very kindly saved me some food for afterwards.

By the time we were done, I gratefully got straight to enjoying the delicious food in the box while sadly Hatti dribbled on everyone with envy.

To compensate Hatti for having had to go without food for several hours, which I'm pretty sure she still hadn't entirely forgiven me for, I decided to treat us both to a day out at the seaside. Having only been together a few months, and with me having had to disappear to the Commonwealth Games for a couple of weeks, we hadn't had a great deal of time to indulge in many leisure activities together, other than going for walks or playing in the garden.

It might sound slightly masochistic, but in the end, I decided we'd go to Edinburgh – almost back to the scene of the crime. My boyfriend at the time was living in nearby Musselburgh, so as well as seeing him, I thought we could spend a few hours on Portobello Beach which I really like. Instead of taking a plane though, we took a train this time. Yes, it took longer, but Hatti and I weren't in any kind of rush and it was nice to just chill out for a while. Hatti got the usual fuss made of her, so she was happy.

After popping in to see my boyfriend for an hour, Hatti and I went straight to the beach. Although she'd had a paddle in a stream or two, I'm pretty sure she'd never been to the sea before, so I was intrigued to see how she'd react. My dad's story about her leaping into the beck had been played out in real life several times both before and since then, so I was aware that she wasn't averse to a paddle and that it could also make her go a little loopy. One of the only times Hatti doesn't do as she's told is when she's off duty and near water, so I knew it would be interesting.

Trying to gauge what she thought of it visually was quite difficult, as when we arrived at the beach, she was her usual impassive self. I could tell she found it interesting though, especially the seagulls. She was smelling the ground, sniffing out chips and bounding about, wagging her tail. They were definitely her kryptonite and I was grateful we didn't live by the sea. As with Dad at the beck, Hatti didn't give me a chance to say, 'Off you go', once her lead was off. She just went for it. The first thing she did was run towards a massive seagull but then she stopped about ten feet away. Hatti may be prone to the odd mad half hour but she's instinctively very sensible and if there's any doubt whatsoever as to whether or not she's in any kind of danger, she'll always err on the side of caution. When it came to the seagull, which was not in the least bit scared of Hatti and would probably have taught her a lesson had she gone any further, she seemed to know full well what this thing was capable of and so kept a safe distance.

Next, Hatti turned her attention to the sea. At first glance, it must have looked more fun than menacing and so she threw caution to the wind and ran in up to her waist. Without warning, the water started to move and a second or so later it was down to her ankles. The look on her face was hilarious. It was 25 per cent confusion and 75 per cent excitement. For the next fifteen minutes or so, she followed the waterline in and out, in and out. To her, the surf, such as it was, was like a giant moving toy which occasionally surprised her by engulfing half her body. Had it been her entire body, that would have been game over.

The difference I notice physically with Hatti when she's off duty is that everything seems to start flopping everywhere, especially her ears and her tongue. It's different somehow to how she is when we we're playing in the garden or going for a walk near home. This seemed to be total relaxation for her and it was lovely to watch.

Once she'd finished playing in the sea, I started chasing her around on the sand and after we'd tired each other out, I got some chips. Having perched myself on a wall facing the sea with Hatti beside me, I ate the chips while she drooled, staring at me with her puppy-dog eyes. Hatti also kept an eye out for seagulls, and it's a good job she did, too, as one or two seemed to think that she and I would be an easy touch for a chip or two. If I hadn't finished them so quickly, I think we'd have been dive-bombed! To this day, that's one of the best times I've ever had with Hatti.

CHAPTER FIVE

FOOD, GLORIOUS FOOD

Like a lot of people, I love a barbecue in the summer and the weekend after our day out to Edinburgh, I decided to have one at home.

The idea, at first, was just to have a few friends over, but it quickly grew into something bigger and before I knew it, I'd invited a flipping gardenfull. I'm not saying I regret that happening, but instead of just popping down to the supermarket and getting a few packs of burgers and sausages and some beers, I had to get a lift down there and fill up somebody's car boot.

For some unknown reason, I hadn't even considered the effect this get-together might have on Hatti, and had I given it even a moment's thought, I'd have sent her away to my mum or dad's. It wasn't the people that worried me – Hatti already knew the vast majority of them and those she didn't know would be joining the queue to say hello and give her some attention. It was the food – or, should I say, the amount of food – that concerned me. Because Hatti is basically a mobile, hairy waste-disposal unit, I knew this was potentially going to play havoc with her, but I was just going to have to keep an eye on her. As well as her potentially overeating, there was going to be a lot of chicken knocking around, so I had to ask my guests that if they were going to give her bits of food – and, let's face it, Hatti was going to make sure they did – not to give her chicken or to give her too much of anything. Most of my guests would probably have known not to give a dog chicken, but you can't be too careful.

As I'd anticipated, when I brought out all the meat from the kitchen, Hatti came trotting over. There was no way in the world I was going to give her any raw meat. I think she knew that, so instead of trying to persuade me to drop something accidentally on purpose, she just sat there drooling. Unlike when there's a piece of apple in the offing and her mouth starts watering, this, on the drool scale, was nothing short of industrial, and after five or ten minutes there was a massive pool of saliva at her feet. In the end, I had to take her indoors as it was putting people off their food.

A couple of days ago, I bought my son, Edward, some cookies from Greggs (cookie was one of his first words!) and when I put them on a plate and gave them to him, Hatti started drooling just like she had at the barbecue. Unfortunately, I only became aware of this when I stepped in a pool of her saliva on my way to the kitchen. I had no shoes or socks on at the time and it felt horrible. What's slightly less disgusting is when she licks her lips. That happens every time she sees, smells or thinks of food, so about every two or three seconds.

Anyway, back to the barbecue. Once I'd finished cooking, I let Hatti out again, and, like any good hostess, she immediately started doing the rounds. (To be fair, even if you don't give her any food, she'll still give you a second or two of her time. She's not in the slightest bit shallow.)

Over the next couple of hours, I tried to keep an eye on Hatti just in case, but everything seemed to be going smoothly. There wasn't any more drooling, which was a relief, and as far as I was aware, she hadn't been given any chicken. I'd also reiterated to my guests once or twice that they should try and ignore her pleas. Even so, I figured that in this situation, even Hatti would get to a point where she just couldn't eat any more titbits or would get fed up having to ask and about twenty minutes later, I saw her go indoors. She was walking like a heavily pregnant elephant and most probably weighed about the same. It could have been the heat, I suppose, but I have a feeling it wasn't!

By way of celebration, I decided to treat myself to a beer. Literally five minutes later, I heard a commotion coming from the direction of the bin at the other end of the garden. People had been putting their leftovers in there and I knew immediately what had happened. When I got there, I found that Hatti, who had obviously discovered a secret stomach, had turned over the bin and was working her way through its contents. The first thing I saw her eat, would you believe, was a piece of chicken on the bone. Well, she didn't exactly eat it. She inhaled it, really. And I now had a potential problem on my hands.

I forget who told me, but at some point in the distant past

somebody mentioned that if a dog eats a chicken bone, you should try and feed them bread as it acts as a binding agent. I think I've got that right. Anyway, I stood there giving Hatti a telling off for being a glutton while she, with her mouth wide open, was fed lots of bread. Talk about sending out mixed messages! In the end, nothing happened (apart from Hatti putting on about a stone). She slept like an absolute log that night. Unlike me – I was too stressed to sleep.

I've had a few barbecues since then, and although I've always managed to keep Hatti chicken-free, she usually manages to coax a few titbits here and there and still does a lovely line in emotional blackmail! The closest she's come to re-enacting Bin-gate was when she pushed off the barbecue lid and started licking the grate. Really, she's got no shame whatsoever!

But on the subject of bins, I used to have one that opened when you touched the lid in a certain place. Such is Hatti's desire to eat at least six times a day and to enjoy as varied a diet as possible that she taught herself how to open the bin. She must have seen me do it hundreds of times and just picked it up. From then on, she was a nightmare. The reason I didn't just buy another one (apart from resenting having to do so) was because I had a feeling that unless it had a padlock on it, or perhaps an armed guard patrolling it, 24 hours a day, seven days a week, she'd eventually crack the code, so to speak. I'm not saying Hatti's super intelligent or anything, but hunger can make you do strange things and in Hatti's case it's opening bins that should really be dog-proof. My mum invested in a similar kind of bin soon after I did, and when Hatti and I visited her one day, I had to tell her what to expect. Sure enough, later that day, Mum went into the kitchen to make a cup of tea and there was Hatti with her nose in the bin gobbling up some old leftovers. Normally, if she's got time, she'll pull the bin over, pull out the bag and go through the entire thing. I've seen her eat a whole lemon before and if there's paper in the bin, she'll eat that too. The phrase 'waste not, want not' could have been coined for her.

Joking aside, I still, to this day, cannot seem to fill Hatti up. I've come close a couple of times (such as at the barbecue), but I have never seen her either refuse food or leave any that's there for the taking. She's just incredible.

Sorry to go on about this so much, but food is clearly as important to Hatti as athletics is to me. Sometimes she'll play Dan and me off each other by pretending she hasn't been fed. If Dan gets home first, he'll feed Hatti and Elmo, and as far as Elmo's concerned, that's it. (He's the opposite of Hatti and although he likes his food, he rarely begs for treats and never asks for more.) If Dan and I are both in the house, she can't get away with it, but if I come home after she and Elmo have been fed, Hatti will look at the cupboard where the food is and sit by her bowl. Sometimes I forget to ask Dan if he's fed them and am led by Hatti's behaviour, but unfortunately for her, Dan will stop me in time. 'Hatti!' he'll say, chasing her out of the kitchen. 'You're nothing but a greedy guts!'

All dogs can do puppy-dog eyes, but when Hatti goes into full-on, 'Help-me-I'm-starving' mode she can almost bring me to tears. Luckily, over the years I've wised up and manage not to fall for her tricks. Honestly. I doubt there are humans who can manipulate on this scale.

And you should see her at train stations. All of a sudden, she'll make a beeline for someone and then sit at their feet, wagging her tail. This has happened countless times over the years and each time I go running over to apologise. The person Hatti's accosted is invariably a dog owner with some treats – or remnants of them – in their coat pocket. It's always a bit embarrassing, but it's also quite impressive, and providing the person has treats (as opposed to remnants), she'll get one.

I had to get drugs-tested last week and no sooner was the lady who was testing me through the door than Hatti was all over her. She was wearing a winter coat and it transpired that it usually had treats in it, but not that day. Miss Piggy was out of luck.

The only thing that's ever disagreed with Hatti – and I mean the *only* thing – is some onion. This too happened at a barbecue at my place and because onion can be poisonous to dogs, I'd put it on the list of things not to give Hatti. I have no idea where or who she got it from but about halfway through the afternoon, I heard her being sick and when I went to investigate I found a small piece of onion. I have to be really careful when I'm chopping onions at home. I'm not the best at doing so, however (I probably shouldn't be doing it at all!), and if a little bit goes flying Hatti will be on it like a flash.

Another food-related incident involving Hatti happened a

couple of weeks ago. I was supposed to be taking Edward out for a picnic and while he was having his morning nap, I made all the sandwiches. I was quite hungry and I knew Edward would be, too, so I made enough to feed a small army. I left the sandwiches on a chopping board on the worktop and went to wake Edward, but when I came down, instead of there being twelve little quarter sandwiches I'd left on the chopping board, there was just one. The chopping board itself had also been moved from the centre of the worktop to the edge. We either had a poltergeist in the house – one that liked sandwiches – or a certain dog had managed to find a way of getting on to the worktop and pulling the chopping board towards her. I still don't know how she managed it, but I found out a few minutes later that she'd also snaffled the sausage rolls.

There are occasions when I'll have to ask people not to feed Hatti at all and my excuse is always that she has a sensitive stomach (I know!) and if she's sick, I'm the one who'll have to clean up the mess. In truth, she could probably digest lead, but they don't know that. I'm just beating Hatti at her own game, manipulating the people she would normally target. She'd kill me if she knew.

I'd like to say that if Hatti was helping me get from A to B she wouldn't deviate if somebody offered her food but I'm afraid that's impossible. Many a time we have been walking through the market only for Hatti to become distracted by a dropped burger or something. And my God, she's quick. That's the part I find most impressive. And there's no point in me saying anything afterwards either; I've tried that and she either ignores me completely or looks at me blankly, as if to say, 'I have absolutely no idea what you're talking about.'

At the end of the day though, everyone has their price and in Hatti's case it starts at half a discarded burger. Or, if she's at the track with me, anybody's packed lunch.

A friend of mine said to me once, 'Libby, there are teeth marks in my tangerine. Do you think that might be Hatti?' It was, and I bet the only reason she hadn't eaten it was because she'd heard somebody coming. I could fill an entire volume with the number of apologies I've had to make to people over the years.

Because I'm a very fussy eater there are times when I could use Hatti as a waste disposal unit. Awards dinners being the most frequent. Quite often I just can't eat what's put in front of me and will sit there looking at Hatti, who will invariably be looking at me if I've got a knife and fork in my hand, wishing I could just tell her to open up and pour it all in! I obviously can't and wouldn't, but it's tempting. As with barbecues, my biggest problem at these events is preventing other people from using Hatti as a waste disposal unit. In fact, I should perhaps have NIL BY MOUTH written along her collar! Edward has been caught feeding her on the odd occasion. If he doesn't like something, rather than tell me, he'll just throw it over the side of his high chair. Sometimes it even lands on Hatti, in which case she'll lick herself clean, but normally it lands in front of her and is gone within seconds.

The best example I have to offer of Hatti not giving two hoots about what goes into her stomach is the time she ate some make-up. I used to have an eyeshadow palette made by a company called Two Faced. It was shaped like a chocolate bar and all the eyeshadows smelled – but didn't taste, as far as I know – of chocolate. Anyway, one day I went into my bedroom to use the palette and found, when I opened it up, that two of the eyeshadows had disappeared. I think I'd only used the thing twice, so unless Dan was keeping a secret from me – quite a big secret – there was an eyeshadow thief in our midst. And given that it looked like they'd been licked away, I suspected Hatti. Who else could it have been?

It's very rare that I catch Hatti in the act but – and I promise I'll move on after this – after the case of the missing eye-shadows I was keeping a close eye on her and saw her wander off in the direction of my bedroom one day. I followed about a minute later, as quietly as I could, peered around the bedroom door and there, before my very eyes, was the guilty party in mid-snaffle. 'Gotcha!' I said making my presence known. 'I knew it was you!' Dogs aren't stupid and if they are discovered doing something they shouldn't, they'll usually try and make up for it by being super nice. A bit like kids, really. When I caught Hatti, that's exactly what she did. She came bounding over to me, tail wagging. 'You little monkey,' I said giving her a stroke. 'Flipping eyeshadow?!'

The only thing that Hatti loves almost as much as food is lying in the sun. And not just for a few minutes. She will literally lie there until her tongue's dry and her heart's going ten to the dozen. We've had some really hot weather recently and I've had to rein her in several times because basically she's been baking herself. And she won't get in a paddling pool to cool down. She'd far sooner carry on toasting.

The first time I realised that Hatti was such a sun goddess was during the very first summer we spent together. I went out for a sunbathe one Sunday afternoon and Hatti followed me. Nothing strange there. She followed me everywhere in those days. After twenty minutes or so – it was absolutely boiling, by the way – I looked around expecting to see that Hatti had gone indoors, but she hadn't. In fact, I could swear she was trying to get a tan.

'Hatti, come on,' I said, giving her tummy a pat and then gesturing for her to follow me. 'Time to go indoors.'

She doesn't often give me evils but when I patted her tummy she gave me a stare that said, 'I suggest you leave me alone!'

'Fair enough,' I said, walking indoors.

Despite the protest, I fully expected Hatti to come lolling in within the next few minutes but after another ten there was still no sign. When I went outside again she was exactly where I'd left her, except this time she was hotter.

'Hatti, come on,' I said. 'Seriously, it's time to come in.'

With that I started gesturing once again for her to follow me indoors but this time, as opposed to giving me evils, she didn't even flinch. Oh my God, I thought. She's been baked alive! After walking over to where she was lying I put my hand very gently on the side of her ribcage. What I'd been hoping to feel was obviously a heartbeat, or at least a sign of life, but what I ended up getting was a burnt hand.

'Flipping heck, Hatti,' I said, pulling my hand away.

This time she flinched, thank God, but before she could complain about the intrusion I got her on her feet and shooed her inside. I could have fried an egg on her back. She was like a black hairy radiator.

Within fifteen minutes she was at the back door again wanting to go back out. 'What, again?' I said to her. 'Ok, you can go out, but only for ten minutes. After that, you're coming back in again. I'm not having dogs roasting in the garden.' Fortunately, the sun went in after about five minutes so she lost interest. It happens all the time though, and unless you literally carry her away she will not budge. The thing is, I always thought dogs hated extreme heat, but I was obviously wrong. Unless Hatti's a one-off, of course, which wouldn't surprise me.

Touch wood, Hatti's only suffered one injury while we've been together. It happened in the autumn after the first barbecue and I don't mind admitting that it put the fear of God into me. We were visiting a place called the Outwoods which comprises some cornfields with a stream running down one side of them. The stream's slightly boggy, which usually results in one of us getting very messy, but it's one of Hatti's favourite places, so whenever I think she's in need of a proper blowout, that's where we go.

Before going in the stream we always have a good old run through the cornfields. This is when Hatti seems to be at her absolute happiest and we only go to the stream once she's properly worn out. This particular visit to the Outwoods had been as enjoyable as ever and it was only when we got back that I realised there was a problem. As Hatti was getting out of the car I noticed that her tail, which usually waves around like a windsock, was curled underneath her body, almost touching her belly button. 'Oh my God,' I said. 'Hatti, what on earth's happened?'

At first, I thought she must have broken her tail at some point during the day and the fact that I hadn't noticed until now made me feel absolutely awful. Also, how was I going to explain this to the people at Guide Dogs? I'd had her less than a year and she'd already broken her tail! What would they say? And what if she could never wag her tail again? Labradors can't have tails that don't wag. It's surely forbidden.

In fact, Hatti could still wag the very end of her tail, which I have to say looked really weird – a bit like a rattlesnake.

I took her to the vet, and the first thing they asked me was how it had happened.

'I had a horrible feeling you were going to ask that,' I said. 'I'm afraid I have no idea. I never heard her yelp at any point. She'd been happy all day.'

It turned out that Hatti had pulled the muscle in her tail, so it looked a lot more serious than it actually was. I suppose I should have realised, as she hadn't been in any pain, but I was too busy panicking. After I explained to the vet what we'd been doing, they arrived at the conclusion that after running around for ages in the cornfields and wagging her tail, the contrast of then jumping into very cold water must have caused the muscle to pull. It was something and nothing, yet I still felt guilty about it.

'How long will it take to get better?' I asked, partly for Hatti's sake and partly in an attempt to quell my guilty conscience.

'It shouldn't take more than a week or so to start getting back to normal,' the vet said.

A week? Every time I looked at Hatti's rattlesnake tail, a swathe of guilt would hit me like a train. And it was so strange-looking that I couldn't stop staring at it.

I ended up ringing the people at Guide Dogs in any case and they just laughed at me. 'It happens all the time,' they said. 'Don't worry about it.'

While we're on the subject of guilt, my all-time favourite Hatti story also involves me going on a bit of a guilt trip. Fortunately, however, it doesn't involve Hatti suffering an injury, minor or otherwise.

I'd moved from my house where I first met Hatti into a bungalow by this time. It was enclosed by a fence and had a nice big garden at the front and back. My partner, Dan, had recently moved in with me and one night, about an hour after getting into bed, I noticed that one of the external security lights had turned on just outside our bedroom, which was next to the front door. A house down the road had a public footpath running parallel to the bottom of the garden and had been targeted several times since we moved in. There'd also been reports of people watching neighbouring properties late at night, so, as you'd expect, everyone was on their guard.

Our hearing tends to compensate for our poor vision (Dan, too, has no central vision and is registered blind) and the previous night, I'd heard somebody in our front garden talking on a mobile phone. I must have scared them off after putting the bedroom light on, and although I didn't actually see them, that had really spooked me.

This time, it was about 11.30 pm when the security light went on and, given what had happened the previous evening, I was jumpy as hell. Consequently, I was also hesitant about getting up to check if anything or anyone was there, so I decided to ask Dan if he'd go. He'd been asleep for about twenty minutes by this point and, by the time I managed to rouse him, the light had gone off again. Just to be on the safe side though, I decided to engage Dan in conversation, to prevent him from falling asleep again too quickly. This paid dividends, as about two minutes later, the light went on again.

'That's the second time it's turned on in the past five minutes,' I said to Dan. 'Not that you'd know. You've been snoring your head off!'

All of a sudden, we heard a noise coming from the front garden where the light was on. With Dan now awake, my bravery suddenly returned and, after jumping out of bed, we both ran to the window and peered through the curtains.

'Can you see anything?' I asked Dan.

'Nope, nothing,' he said. 'You?'

'Not a thing.'

Just then the security light went on again.

'What should we do?' I said to Dan. 'There's definitely somebody in the garden.'

The first thing we did was run around the house looking out of all the windows.

Again, neither of us saw anything.

Then, one of the security lights at the back of the house went on and, a few seconds later, the one at the front went on again. Oh my God, I thought. We're under attack!

Dan suffers from something called cone-rod dystrophy, which, like my condition, runs in his family and he only has about 3 per cent vision. Mine's only slightly better than Dan's though, so regardless of how many security lights we had placed around the house, we weren't going to be able to see very much at all, and especially through tiny gaps in the curtains.

Nevertheless, we came to the conclusion that rather than being attacked by humans, who even we would have been able to see when the security lights were on, we were actually being attacked by an army of rabid foxes. This took some of the fear away from the situation, but with the lights still going on and off all the time we wondered what they were after.

When the light next to the front door went on again a minute or two later, Dan looked through the letter box.

'I think I can see one of them,' he said. 'Yes, I can. It's about three or four metres away. It's just sitting there.'

'Try scaring it,' I said.

'How?' asked Dan.

'Shout at it.'

'It's after midnight. I can't start shouting now.'

'I don't mean loudly.'

'All right, keep your hair on,' said Dan. 'I'll give it a go.'

He opened the letter box again, checked to make sure the fox was still there – which it was – and, putting his mouth to the opening, he said, 'Hey, you, bugger off! Go on, bugger off!'

'Has it gone?' I asked.

'Erm, no,' said Dan, looking again. 'I'm afraid not.'

What alarmed us slightly was the fact that foxes are usually very wary of humans, yet this one didn't seem to give a monkey's. A fox without fear? Surely that could be potentially dangerous? A killer on the loose . . .

'Why don't I try throwing something at it?' said Dan after having a think.

'That's a good idea,' I said. 'What have we got that's small and hard?'

'How about potatoes?' Dan suggested.

'Haven't got any in. And besides, that's food. It'll think we want to adopt it!'

After having another think, we decided to try shooing it away using an unravelled wire coat hanger. We were going to use a broom, but that was outside, so this would have to do.

When Dan looked through the letter box again, the fox had moved forward slightly. 'It's standing up now,' he said. 'Before, it was sitting down.'

Dan tried in vain for about five minutes to scare the fox away using the coat hanger and whispered intermittent cries of, 'Go on. Go away.' It was no use though. The fox was not for buggering off.

By this time, I'd moved from the hall into the living room and, after giving up the ghost with the coat hanger, Dan joined me.

'I'm surprised this hasn't woken Hatti up,' he said sitting down. 'She's usually a light sleeper.'

At that moment, we looked at each other. 'Hatti!' we said together. 'She's the bloody fox!'

Dan and I ran back to the front door.

'I must have forgotten to let her in and lock up,' I said. Normally, I let Hatti out for a final pee before brushing my teeth and then, once I've finished, I'll let her back in again and lock up. On this occasion, however, I must have been distracted by something.

Whenever I tell people this story, the question they usually ask at this point is why didn't Hatti bark at all? Hatti hardly ever barks, except when she's telling another dog off. Seriously, I've never known a dog as quiet as Hatti, which is another reason why I'm always falling over her. Generally speaking, Labradors and Retrievers aren't especially barky dogs, but it's as though she's taken a vow of silence or something.

I genuinely can't remember the last time Hatti barked. It's that rare. And it can be quite infuriating sometimes, as when someone is at the door, Hatti makes no noise whatsoever and doesn't even get up. What self-respecting dog doesn't go bananas when the front doorbell rings or when the postman comes? Sometimes, if I'm in the garden, I won't hear the doorbell and I get no help from her at all. I dread to think what she'd be like if we ever did have an intruder. Bloody useless!

Anyway, sure enough, the front door was unlocked and when Dan pulled it open, there, standing about two metres in front of us, was Hatti. Of course, it's wrong to try and humanise dogs (like dressing them up as superheroes, ahem), but they do experience a lot of what humans do, and the look on Hatti's face when she walked into the light was pure pity. You poor, unfortunate idiots, she was obviously thinking – or something like that. Boy, did we feel guilty though, not to mention stupid. We laugh about it now but it took us ages to tell somebody what had happened! Thank goodness dogs can't talk.

Hatti's other 'looks', apart from, 'Help me, I'm starving' and, 'Really, Libby?' (the one she gives me when I try and dress her up), include a kind of, 'Yeah, whatever' look (this she does if I'm telling her off – it's pure defiance), a nonchalant, bored look (also when I'm telling her off or if she wants to move on from somewhere), a sideways glance (when she's being playful, meaning, I think, something like, 'Go on then, tickle me') and last, but not least, her famous eyebrow raiser, which comes straight from the Roger Moore school of acting and denotes surprise. Actually, I've forgotten one. When Edward was very small, he wasn't very good at doing what we now call 'the gentle stroke' and could sometimes be rough with Hatti. Her look in that situation meant two words: save me!

I've now retired from trying to dress Hatti up and, as far as she's concerned, it's not before time. To her, it's a crime against dogmanity and if she had the wherewithal to do so, she'd undoubtedly start a petition to get it banned. I can't always see when Hatti's displeased (that's my excuse and I'm sticking to it) and the first time I realised that fancy dress might not be her thing was when I was squinting at a photo one day. In it, she'd managed to express displeasure and disgust in one steely glance and after seeing it I vowed never to do it again.

The closest I get now to influencing Hatti sartorially is when I buy her a new collar, the only trouble being that whenever we find a nice one, she'll immediately go and cover it in fox poo. The dilemma I have with Hatti is that people often mistake her for a boy. It'd be so tempting to counter this by giving her an overtly 'girly' collar (I've seen dogs with diamanté collars and leads before), but I always manage to resist. She's definitely not a girly girl and currently, she's sporting a very nice Harris tweed one that I bought online. She looks traditional and quite elegant, and while I wasn't sure at first, I think the Harris tweed works – if Hatti were a human, she'd definitely be a country girl.

In any case, although I can't see very well, I'm usually very attuned to Hatti's expressions, which help to keep me abreast of how she's feeling. It's not an exact science, of course, but Hatti's emotional wellbeing is very important to me, so even an inkling of what's going on is useful. I often find a good bum scratch brings her back to life if she's feeling a bit down. And I'm always happy to oblige.

CHAPTER SIX

HATTI'S PEOPLE

One of Hatti's most endearing qualities, which became apparent from the get-go and can still cause the odd problem now and then, is her friendliness. Hatti genuinely has more friends than I do, and they're scattered all over the land. Surprisingly, the crux of these relationships isn't always food, although it's often involved.

I think I said earlier that the general public tend to gravitate towards guide dogs. At first, I assumed that this would lead to conversation with me. You know: 'Ooh, isn't she lovely? You don't mind me stroking her, do you? What's her name? Have you had her long?' That sort of thing. And it does occur from time to time. But what happens more regularly is people giving Hatti lots of attention, while either ignoring me altogether or using me as an information desk. I'm usually asked what her name is and from then on, I'm surplus to requirements. Far from being put out by this, I find it hilarious and over the years, I've had to break up literally hundreds of love-ins. 'Excuse me,' I'll say, very apologetically. 'Would you mind if I have her back? We have a train to catch.' Nine times out of ten my request will be met with a mixture of apologies and thanks.

On the rare occasion when it becomes a three-way thing, with Hatti getting lots and lots of attention, as the person simultaneously chats to me, we could be there for at least half an hour, depending on our schedules. In the early days, I used to find ending these meetings difficult, as I was afraid of appearing rude. Also, Hatti often gets approached by older people and I always have a horrible feeling that they might be lonely. The catalyst for me becoming more ruthless in these situations was when a woman kept me chatting for over an hour one day, and I really did end up missing a train. I must have tried twenty or thirty times to make our excuses, but the lady just carried on talking. I vowed from that day on to be more assertive and armed myself with a list of excuses, the pick of which was, 'You'll have to excuse us. She's had really bad diarrhoea and we're due at the vet's in five minutes.' That usually clears the way, so to speak.

One of the reasons why people are so attracted to Hatti, and to dogs in general, is because they don't judge like we do. Social media has made it easier than ever for people to judge one another, so being able to spend time with 'somebody' who is pleased to see you, with no strings attached, even for just a minute or two, is a blessing. I often hear people say that they prefer the company of dogs to people and, in some cases, I can see why. It all depends on what kind of mood you're in, I suppose. Or at least it does with me. The difference being that I never tire of seeing Hatti or spending time with her, whereas with humans I do.

One of the most useful things to come from Hatti's popularity involves my inability to see people's faces, as I've mentioned. Sometimes somebody will approach us who I've known for absolutely ages, yet unless I can see them clearly I might not recognise them, and I can only see them clearly if they're quite close . They'll invariably know Hatti so the way I get around this is by saying something along the lines of, 'Hello! Look who's here, Hatti.' And then they'll hopefully say something like, 'Hello! Do you remember me, Hatti? Of course you do. It's Mary, isn't it? Now then. Have I got a treat for you? I'm sure I've got some somewhere. Yes, here we are.' I'll then re-join the conversation, confident in the knowledge that I know who I'm talking to and won't appear rude: 'How are you, Mary? What have you been up to?'

Another thing guide dogs are especially good at is acting as ice breakers. This is similar to the above scenario, but without them necessarily being the centre of attention. The first time I realised how effective a guide dog's presence was in helping to foster social niceties was while we were on a train to Edinburgh. We were sitting at a table with two other people who were obviously travelling separately and when we first sat down the atmosphere was a bit stuffy. You know what it's like when you're sitting with two or three strangers. Everyone's precious about how much table the other people are taking up and about what they're reading or looking at on their laptops.

When I sat down on the train to Edinburgh with Hatti you could almost feel the tension evaporate and the people start to relax. The person sitting directly opposite me, who was a man in his forties (I think), started asking me about Hatti and, within about five minutes, the three of us (the other person was a woman who was probably in her fifties) were all chatting away like old friends. For the first ten minutes or so, Hatti was the topic of conversation, then we drifted from person to person and from subject to subject. It ended up being one of the most enjoyable train journeys I've ever had and at the end of the day, it was all thanks to Hatti.

Funnily enough, the chap who first started talking to me on that train assumed that I was Hatti's trainer. This is quite common and stems from the misapprehension I once also had about guide dogs being used mainly by older people. It also means that the conversation starts off with me as opposed to her; but once they realise that she's fully trained and working, it tends to revert to her again. What I've learned to appreciate over the years is that the vast majority of conversations I've had in Hatti's presence, certainly with strangers, have been instigated because of her, so Hatti being the centre of attention, more often than not, is fine by me.

My favourite situation when it comes to meeting strangers is when parents approach me on behalf of their children. What usually happens is that a child will come up to Hatti and then the mum or dad will pull them away. 'No, no,' they'll say. 'That's a special dog. You can't touch it.' This then pushes me into saying something like, 'No, don't worry. Hatti loves kids.' Which she does. Sometimes the parent won't notice until their child has already made contact with Hatti and if that happens, panic will normally ensue. 'Oh my God, I'm so sorry!' they'll say, pulling their child away. Once I've placated the parent, I'll then invite them and the child to formally meet Hatti, and while they're giving her some welcome attention, I'll take the opportunity to dispel a few myths and tell them a bit about how guide dogs work. The kids absolutely love meeting Hatti. It makes them feel quite special, and you know for a fact that as soon as they see their friends, she's all they're going to talk about. The line that always impresses them most is when I say that Hatti helps me to see. 'Really?' they'll say, open-mouthed. 'That's amazing!' To a three- or four-year-old child that's probably mind-bending, and although I can't see them very well, I can imagine the expressions on their faces.

One of the most noticeable differences between the relationship a normal dog owner might have with a pet and the relationship a blind person has with a guide dog is how we're perceived by other people. Because we're usually joined at the hip, literally, Hatti and I are basically one entity in some people's eyes and the thought of saying either of our names on their own just wouldn't work. We are, Libby and Hatti, or Hatti and Libby, whichever you prefer.

The acid test as to which of us has made the biggest impression is if I meet an acquaintance, as in somebody who Hatti and I have met once or twice before but isn't a friend, when I'm on my own. It probably won't surprise you to learn that the question these people always ask first is, 'Where's Hatti?' and I honestly can't remember more than a couple of occasions where they've remembered who I am. Usually they just avoid having to ask me and once I've told them where Hatti is and that she's fine they usually make their excuses and go. Honestly, the amount of times I've been left standing there like a lemon after telling somebody who can't remember my name that Hatti's fit and well.

The reason I'm ok with it is because I do exactly the same thing! I shudder to think how many blind people I've been introduced to over the years and if I meet them for a second time, nine times out of ten I'll remember the name of the guide dog but not them. Appalling, isn't it?

The most bizarre encounter I've ever experienced with Hatti on a train involved another guide dog. We were on our way from Loughborough to Nottingham, so it was only a short train ride and the train itself was just a couple of carriages. Hatti seemed quite agitated when we boarded and instead of going right, which is where my seat was and where I'd commanded her to go, she wanted to go left. I assumed there must have been somebody nearby holding a McDonald's or something, and disregarding her behaviour I commanded her to go right again and she did as she was told. After sitting down, I took off Hatti's harness and lead for a moment, but before I could see if she was ok, she'd disappeared under the seat. Hatti can be erratic sometimes, but she'd never done anything like this before and as I stood up and started panicking, she began combat crawling underneath the seats and down the carriage. 'Hatti,' I shouted. 'Hatti, come out of there, now!' I walked into the aisle and tried following her down the carriage. This was quite hard as I was doing it by sound, but after passing what must have been seven or eight rows of seats, I spotted the object of her endeavours. It was another guide dog, who I soon found out was called Richie, and about five seconds later, Hatti appeared from under the seat beside him and started saying hello. Debbie from Guide Dogs had told me that it's the harness they recognise and sometimes they'll try and make friends.

Both Richie's owner (a lady called Emma Bullen who I still see from time to time) and I were embarrassed, but she very kindly invited me and Hatti to sit with them and the four of us soon became friends. Hatti had never been this unpredictable before and it took me by surprise at first. But the fact that guide dogs actually recognise and acknowledge each other is really sweet and it's become another of my favourite Hatti stories.

Another guide dog that springs to mind who Hatti became quite keen on turned out not to be a fan of female dogs, so unfortunately, her advances weren't reciprocated. Hatti didn't seem to notice though, to be honest, which either makes her very thick-skinned or a bit daft.

One of the most surprising friendships Hatti has made is with a dog called Megan who belongs to Dan's parents. When they first got Megan from an animal-rescue centre they were told that she hadn't mixed much with other dogs and could therefore be quite aggressive with them. In an effort to avoid confrontation, Dan's parents made a conscious decision to keep Megan away from other dogs as much as possible. They walked her at times when they knew other dog walkers wouldn't be about and were generally very careful.

When Dan invited me over to meet his parents for the first time, he worried what might happen between Megan and Hatti. But at the end of the day, she had to come with me, so we were just going to have to hope for the best. By this point, Megan hadn't socialised with another dog for almost ten years, so it could very easily have been a disaster. The worst-case scenario going forward would have been having to keep them apart at every meeting, and although that wouldn't have been the end of the world, I didn't want my first ever meeting with Dan's parents to end up in a dog fight, so to speak.

I forget whose idea it was, but after arriving at the house, the first thing we did was to take Hatti and Megan out for a walk. I was already nervous about meeting Dan's parents for the first time without having this to worry about as well, but as soon as we got out of the car Megan came running over to Hatti and from then on, they were inseparable. I'm certainly no dog psychiatrist, but if I were to hazard a guess, I'd say that because Hatti's very placid she probably doesn't give off many threatening or aggressive vibes. This happy turn of events helped me, Dan and his parents to relax and we've hated each other ever since. Only joking! For Dan's parents it was a huge relief though. I think they'd spent a lot of time worrying about Megan over the years, and to see her mixing happily with another dog must have been a joy. Since then, Megan has become a more social animal and has lots of dog friends that she sees every day of the week. It's been a happy beginning for Dan's parents and Megan and was a happy beginning for Dan's parents and me, I'm pleased to say.

Megan isn't the only dog that Hatti has helped bring out of their shell. One of our friends has a dog called Max who is a white Retriever cross. When he first arrived, Max was pretty anxious around other dogs. They got him from a rescue centre, so it's not too surprising. The poor thing had obviously had some bad experiences and you could tell that he'd suffered. One day, Max ended up meeting Hatti and Elmo on a walk, and, just like it had with Megan, it seemed to have this miraculous effect on him. He didn't suddenly become the most confident dog on the planet, but whenever Hatti and Elmo were around him, he'd find another layer. They even formed a bit of a pack on walks together. It was brilliant. However, poor Max often used to attract the wrong kind attention on these walks and while he, Elmo and Hatti were all playing together, other dogs would come over and try mounting him. Poor Max! I don't know what it is about him (he must give off some kind of irresistible smell or something), but it became something of a regular blush on a walk.

One day, Hatti and I were out for a walk with Max and his owner and within five minutes another dog had started chasing him. We could tell from experience that this dog had more on its mind than just a game of chase and we were readying ourselves to rescue Max – again! But what happened next took me completely by surprise. As soon as the other dog started chasing Max, Hatti chased it off. I'd seen her being protective before, but this was on a different scale and when the dog carried on chasing Max, Hatti started barking. Not just barking, but *really* barking. As I said earlier, this was a really rare occurrence and a sign that Hatti meant business. She was basically telling this dog that if it didn't clear off right now and leave her friend alone, she'd have its guts for garters. It took a few seconds, but the dog finally got the message and fled. And Hatti didn't stop barking at it or chasing until it was about a hundred metres away. It was obviously her version of a restraining order and it worked an absolute treat. I'd never seen her react like that to anything before and she hasn't done it since. For the rest of the walk, she didn't let Max out of her sight and no other dogs came near him. So much for giving off non-threatening and non-aggressive vibes. She was magnificent.

My sister, Felicity, is a veterinary nurse and her dog is a proper little gremlin. One day, a French Bulldog puppy was brought into her surgery with all kinds of problems. It was born via C-section and sadly had a really bad cleft palate. The breeder was concerned he would die without nursing care and my sister decided that he could come and live with her and she would hand rear him. Her initial idea was to nurse the puppy to health and then, when it was old enough, have it rehomed. As you might expect, she ended up falling in love with him after about five minutes and has now had him for over three years. He's called Forrest, by the way, as in, Gump, and is incredibly boisterous.

Forrest is what we humans would call very spoilt and is always trying to prove a point. This is very common with hand rears as he hasn't had a mother teaching him dog behaviour and how to read other dogs, so he has to learn by trial and error. When he first met Hatti, who isn't massive, but is a lot bigger than him, he set about trying to goad her into a play fight. Regardless of how hard Forrest tried though, Hatti was having none of it. He tried nipping her ears and then her legs. He tried everything. In the end, Hatti turned around and gave young Forrest a proper barking at and, as you might expect, that did the trick. He's still a pain in the bum sometimes, but he thinks the absolute world of Hatti and they get on like a house on fire. She's like a big sister to him.

It's quite strange but when it comes to members of my family – and their dogs – it's almost as if Hatti knows we're related and she acts differently towards them. I expect that's quite a common trait with dogs. We're not a massively tactile family, and we probably don't act too differently to how we act around friends, but Hatti definitely knows the difference. My brother Stephen comes to stay with us sometimes for a week or two at a time and the first time he arrived, Hatti was all over him. It was as though she'd known him for ever. Despite being friendly, she usually takes a little time to warm up, regardless of who it is, but with my brother there was none of that. There's so much about dogs that we don't know . . .

Somebody asked me the other day if Hatti has a favourite person (apart from me, of course!) and after thinking about it for a few seconds (and taking away the food element), I answered that it's probably a lady called Ronnie who was our next-door neighbour when we lived in the bungalow. I hadn't had Hatti all that long when we moved in there and Ronnie, who is in her early seventies now and undoubtedly one of the friendliest people I've ever met, immediately offered to have Hatti whenever I had to go away. She is the person Hatti has spent the most amount of time with other than me, but because Ronnie doesn't work her, their relationship is based purely around leisure. The daily routine at Ronnie's involves food, walks, play and naps. That's for both of them, by the way.

It won't surprise you to learn that this relationship was born of Ronnie coming around to the bungalow when we first moved in and giving Hatti treats. After a while, Ronnie got wise to the fact that I didn't like her giving Hatti too many treats, and would claim that they were just tiny bits of dog food and were very good for her. Looking back, I'm pretty sure I was hoodwinked by the two of them, but I can't prove anything. Lord only knows what happens when I'm not there.

Speaking of Hatti and Ronnie, it was during one of those early "holidays" at Ronnie's house that I first realised just how much Hatti meant to me. There'd been a few little things before that which had made me feel quite protective towards her but this was on a different scale.

I was competing in Germany at the time and was going to be over there for the best part of a week. On day two, I think it was, while in my hotel room, I suddenly felt an almost overwhelming desire to see Hatti. Not for practical reasons. In fact, I'd been coping fine without her, thanks to some help from my guide runner. I just really, really missed her.

This was probably one of the first times I'd been away from Hatti for more than a day or two since she'd come to live with me and as well as missing her terribly, I started remembering all the things we'd done together. It was almost an epiphany, in a way. A sudden surge of appreciation. Unfortunately, this was quickly replaced by an avalanche of worry, which was something else that hadn't happened before. I knew that Ronnie would be taking good care of Hatti but it's like having children, in the sense that, in your mind at least, nobody can look after them as well as you can. Long-term, the most important lesson I learned from this experience was to ask as few questions as possible of the person doing the looking after as the more you know, the more likely you are to worry. As long as you know they're ok, that's the main thing, and if they are, leave it there. In the end I rang Ronnie and asked her if she'd send me a photo of Hatti, which she very kindly did. As well as putting my mind at rest, it just made me feel better. That's just the effect she has on me, and I expect she always will.

Asking whoever's looking after Hatti to send me a photo or a video of her has become a habit now and it's something I ask as a matter of course. I don't know how she did it, but while I was away competing a few years ago my mum managed to get Hatti to hold a piece of paper in her mouth with Good Luck written on it!

To this day, if I have to go to London, for instance, and think I can cope without Hatti, she'll go and stay with Ronnie. There aren't too many places I can't take Hatti, but London's always very busy, and as well as being short on space there, we often have trouble finding places where Hatti can go to the loo.

Whenever I get back from London, or if I've been abroad, Ronnie will give me a rundown of what she and Hatti have been up to. As I just said, it's normally a conveyor belt of walks, play, food, and naps, and the sentence, 'I enjoyed having Hatti for her company in the garden' also makes an appearance now and then. Unfortunately, Ronnie's husband died a couple of years ago and during the first lockdown in 2020, Hatti went to stay with her for a fortnight just to keep her company. We were also trying to move to a new house, which is where we are living now, so it worked well for all of us. But especially for Hatti. She hates upheaval and I seem to remember there being a fair amount of that at the time. Together with Edward, she's always my first consideration when I have to make big decisions and if I think she might suffer in any way I'll always make sure she's out of the way.

In the year or so following that move, which has been spent mainly in lockdown, Hatti has continued to see Ronnie on a regular basis and two or three times a week they'll go out for a stroll together. I think the lives of most people will have been curtailed somehow since Covid struck and although Hatti has almost perfected the art of doing nothing she's definitely needed a change of surroundings. As has Ronnie. I'm not saying familiarity has bred any contempt but, at the risk of mixing my metaphors, you can also have too much of a good thing! In Ronnie's case, it's mainly been about company and because of the restrictions it's been hard for her, as I'm sure it has for millions of other people.

I can't think of a better substitute for human company than a dog. In fact, there are studies being conducted all the time and all over the world these days into the effects that dogs can have on the lives of humans and right at the top of the list, together with assisting people with disabilities, is helping to stave off loneliness. One of the latest studies I heard about took place in Australia last year and found that after just one month of owning a dog, people who had previously experienced severe loneliness were much happier and experienced far fewer negative emotions. There were also suggestions in the study that dogs could help to reduce blood pressure in humans, which didn't surprise me. I expect they can also raise people's blood pressure, in fact I know they can, but what I also know is that the benefits must outweigh the negatives a hundred to one.

By far the most unwelcome offer of friendship Hatti has ever received came from a male Labrador. She and I were on our way back from the track one day when, all of a sudden, this Labrador came bounding up behind Hatti and tried to give her an uninvited cuddle. Hatti was absolutely disgusted, as was the owner of the randy Labrador.

'I'm so sorry,' he said to me. 'He's not normally like that.'

I found it funny and accepted his apology – the poor man was mortified.

At that moment, the excited Labrador who wouldn't take no for an answer, tried again, but this time Hatti was ready for him, as was the owner. 'Come here,' he said, pulling the dog towards him. After the owner apologised to me again, and to Hatti, the Labrador had yet another go at forcing his attentions on her. He'd obviously taken quite a shine to Hatti and I gave him ten out of ten for persistence! Unlike Hatti. This time, she just sat down and turned away from him, as if to say, 'There's no way you're coming near me, mate'. After that, both owner and Labrador went on their way and we went on ours.

About a minute later, I heard the Labrador owner's voice again in the distance. 'Spot,' he was shouting. 'Come here, Spot!'

I turned around and there, running towards us at full pelt, was Spot, with his tongue sticking out and a very flustered owner following some way behind. Young Spot was obviously very good off the lead as a rule, and once the owner thought they were a safe distance away from Spot's new love interest – or should I say, lust interest – he must have let him off again. What a mistake!

As soon as Hatti saw Spot coming, she sat down and turned the other way, which I suppose was her version of locking the bedroom door behind her. As we waited for Spot's owner to catch up with us, I stood guard in front of Hatti and tried calming Spot down. He was actually a lovely dog and had I been matchmaking that day – and had Hatti been interested – I'd have taken her to one side and told her that she could do a lot worse. Hatti didn't bark at him, which is how she usually tells other dogs off, so perhaps she wasn't too disgusted after all?

When Spot's poor owner finally arrived, he was as red as a beetroot – part embarrassment and part exhaustion – and after getting Spot back on his lead again, he repeated his apologies. 'It won't happen again,' he said, looking at me and then at Hatti. 'I'll keep him on his lead until we get home. I promise!'

CHAPTER SEVEN

TOO MANY DOGS!

Just about the only thing that's easier with a white cane than it is with a guide dog is taking a taxi. With black cabs it isn't a problem. In fact, black-cab drivers are some of the most helpful people I've come across since getting Hatti and I've never once been let down. But with minicabs it's a different story, and I could be wrong, but I'd say that's primarily down to knowledge – or lack of it. Black-cab drivers know exactly what's expected of them when it comes to taking passengers – especially with different needs – and although you shouldn't tar everyone with the same brush, that doesn't seem to be the case with minicab drivers.

One of my worst experiences was in Manchester in 2018. Dan was appearing as a contestant on the TV show *Ninja Warrior UK*, so he was there with Elmo and I was there with Hatti. After Dan had taken part in the competition, somebody from the production company ordered us a taxi back to the train station. 'Please make sure they're aware that we have guide dogs with us,' I said. Taxis are obliged to take guide dogs by law, but many try to refuse, so I thought it best to make sure we got a driver who was both aware of this and compliant.

When the taxi arrived, a runner from the production company showed us to the exit and as we approached the car, we suddenly heard a clicking sound.

'Has he just locked his doors?' I asked Dan.

'I think he has,' he replied.

Dan knocked on the driver's window and signalled for him to wind it down, which he did. 'Why have you locked the doors?' I asked the driver.

'No dogs,' he said sharply.

'But these are working dogs,' I replied. 'And unless you're exempt because of an allergy and can prove it to me here and now, you're obliged to take them by law.'

'I don't care,' said the driver, who was now getting quite stroppy. 'I don't want dogs in my taxi and that's that. Find another one.'

Dan and I had been up since the crack of dawn and the last thing I wanted was an argument. Even so, I was damned if I was going to let this one go. So, I took out my phone and took a photograph of the registration number, then went to have another word with him.

'Right then,' I began. 'If you refuse to take us, I'm going to report you to the council, and they will have to revoke your licence. Once that's happened, I'll bring a private prosecution. You've got two choices: you either take us to the train station or I report you and then prosecute you. And I will! Now, what's it to be?'

I'm honestly not a very confrontational person normally, but everyone has their limits. This man was being ignorant and I wanted him to realise what his responsibilities were.

'Ok,' he said gruffly. 'I'll take you.'

Guide dogs just sit quietly in the footwell in a cab and are probably far less bother than many human passengers. I'm not sure if this had been explained to the driver when he took his taxi-driver course (or if they even have to do one), but once he realised this was the case, he attempted a half-hearted reconciliation. I was so wound up by this point, however, that I'm afraid I was having none of it. His attitude was awful from the get-go and it was going to take a lot more than, 'I suppose they're not too bad, after all,' for me to want to forgive him.

Despite the fact that he eventually relented, I could still have had him prosecuted for the initial refusal and I told him so in no uncertain terms. I'd also filmed the latter half of the exchange on my mobile, so I was taking no prisoners. I actually surprised myself as Dan would normally be the one to do any arguing. I was like a woman possessed!

By the time we got to the train station, I'd softened, and the driver genuinely seemed to be sorry. He was also visibly surprised at how well behaved and quiet Hatti and Elmo had been and so we parted on good terms. There aren't many things in life that have such a dramatic effect on my emotional state, but taxi drivers refusing to take guide dogs and their owners is definitely one of them.

I have had somebody champion this cause on my behalf

before, and boy, did he go for it. Once again it was in Manchester. The Trafford Centre, to be exact. I was queueing for a taxi to go to my sister's house, which isn't too far away, and when it was my turn, the man who was in charge of the taxi rank gestured to the next driver to pull forward. When he didn't do so, the man in charge went to talk to the driver and I knew exactly what the problem was. The driver was pointing at Hatti and he obviously didn't want to take us.

I'm not sure what I was expecting to happen next but what came to pass was a complete surprise. The man in charge let rip at this taxi driver in his very broad Mancunian accent and basically issued the same threat as I had, in that if he didn't do as he'd been asked, he'd be reported to the council. The driver capitulated immediately and within seconds, Hatti and I were being shown into the cab by my knight in shining armour. Or, in this case, jeans and a bomber jacket. 'There you are, love,' he said, opening the taxi door. 'Sorry about that. You'll have no more trouble from him. He'll be as good as gold.'

Just as on the other occasion, the driver went overboard trying to be nice to me as we set off, but I made it clear that I didn't want to be in his taxi any more than he wanted to take me, and I arrived at my sister's in a stinking mood. Some time after this, I came across a taxi driver who not only didn't mind taking Hatti, but actually seemed to enjoy it and on top of that he was really nice and great company. I'd been trying to get a cab in Loughborough one day, and once I'd reached the front of the queue at the taxi rank (which isn't manned like the one at the Trafford Centre), two drivers saw me and just drove off. The next driver to arrive fortunately stopped, and as well as getting out to open the door for me, which normally only black-cab drivers do, he was also very chatty. This was a relief, as I was on my way to London to appear on a TV show called *The Wright Stuff* and given that the drive would take between two and a half and three hours (or so I thought), the last thing I wanted from the company was a moody bloke who didn't like dogs.

The driver told me his name was Jakki (a name he uses because his real name is difficult to pronounce, I believe) and that he was originally from Bangladesh. Jakki admitted straight away that, as a devout Muslim, he was always nervous about taking guide dogs, but as well as being obliged to do so, he appreciated how difficult it must be for the person travelling. I thought that was so sweet of him. The journey ended up taking almost six hours, so Jakki and I had plenty of time to talk and get acquainted. He was very interested in guide dogs because they don't have them in Bangladesh. He also told me a lot about his culture and, in particular, why Muslims consider dogs to be dirty. I found this interesting, but I'm afraid I don't consider it grounds for anyone to refuse to take a guide dog. After that journey, instead of having to suffer the ignominy of standing in a queue at a taxi rank and being ignored by drivers, I would just call up Jakki whenever I needed a cab and he would take me instead. Problem solved. From a financial point of view, it worked out well for him, too, as sometimes I can be really busy, and, as with my trip to London, I might need to travel hundreds of miles in a day. The news that Jakki had become my personal chauffeur ended up filtering down to his taxi friends and a few of them were really envious.

When Jakki moved to Newcastle in the spring of 2020, I was gutted. We'd become good friends and he'd kept Hatti and me entertained for hours on end. Fortunately, a cousin of his stepped into the breach and, I'm happy to say, he's just as nice and just as accommodating.

One of my favourite trips with Jakki was the time he took Hatti and me to Crufts. I was being sponsored by a dog-food brand called Eukanuba at the time – or should I say Hatti was? – and they'd invited us up there for the day. I was booked to give a talk about my relationship with Hatti and to be interviewed, and although I'd heard of Crufts and had seen the *Best in Show* on television once or twice while running around the arena, I had no idea what to expect.

Paradoxically, the first shock I got on arriving there was that people are allowed to take their dogs with them. I thought Crufts was just for show dogs and had no idea it was basically a canine free-for-all. After thinking about it for a second though, it made perfect sense: millions of doggy products being sold by hundreds of companies to thousands of dog owners.

But in all seriousness, I was quite overwhelmed by this, as was Hatti. Not in a bad way. We just hadn't been expecting to see thousands of dogs that day. Also, the sheer size of the show was incredible. I've been to the Paralympic Games three times, but this was off the scale. I don't mean in terms of numbers of people (and dogs). I mean the incredible atmosphere. At the Paralympic and Olympic Games, there are people supporting different countries and people who are interested in certain sports. At Crufts, it's the opposite. Or kind of. Everyone there is dog mad. That's a given. But you also get the feeling that everyone's on show, not just some of the dogs. I suppose it makes sense. After all, Crufts is the biggest dog show on the planet. If you're there as an exhibitor, you're on show and if you're there as a customer with a dog in tow, you'll want to show them off, too. That's the impression I got at Crufts. It's a show in every single respect.

You know they say that dogs sometimes look like their owners? Well, at Crufts that's taken to another level – there were people whose dogs were dressed up in exactly the same kind of clothing as them and some had even dyed their hair the same colour as their dog's (and vice versa) and had matching accessories. I may only have peripheral vision, but even I felt embarrassed by the fact that I couldn't stop staring. When all's said and done though, people only do this because they love their dogs, and I think that's sweet. I'm not sure it would work with me and Hatti though. She'd look ridiculous in shorts, vest and trainers and yellow harnesses have never really suited me.

Once I'd got over the fact that there were so many dogs there I then marvelled at the number of different breeds. At the time, I was on first-name terms with several Labradors, a French Bulldog, a couple of Jack Russells and one or two mutts, but I'd never seen so many breeds close up, let alone how they all behaved. Unfortunately, it was behaviour that became our undoing. Hatti was probably the only working dog there that day (working dogs are Day 3 at Crufts and we were there on Day 5) and, consequently, she became something of a curiosity. It seemed like every single dog there wanted to sniff and make friends with her and I could tell that she was beginning to get flustered, bless her. Had she been off duty, I dare say she'd have had a ball, but she's a professional through and through is Hatti, and despite the unwanted attention, she managed to remain focused. How, I have absolutely no idea, but she was as cool as a cucumber.

On a positive note, wherever there are dogs and dog owners with lots of cash there are always lots of free samples to be had, and the sheer quantity of freebies on offer reached biblical proportions. Those who weren't trying to sell collars and other accessories were trying to sell food of some kind and Hatti was in her absolute element. It also helped her to concentrate, I think, and made me feel better about taking her there. It was compensation.

Because it was so busy, I don't remember too much about what we had to do that day. My fellow sprinter Iwan Thomas did a question-and-answer session with me and Hatti on the Eukanuba stand and we also did some filming. Hatti tried walking off the stage during the Q&As. Not because of anything Iwan said – he was great – but, like any dog, Hatti's boredom threshold is far from infinite and when it reaches its natural end, she feels compelled to act. This usually involves her simply walking off and having a quick change of scene for a few minutes, but when you're both sitting on a stage in front of several hundred people it can be quite amusing. It's happened a few times over the years and it always gets a laugh. Dogs have fantastic comic timing.

On one occasion, about a year ago, I was asked to make a speech at a meeting for the Guide Dogs charity. I forget what the event was in aid of, but all the charity's bigwigs were there, so it must have been quite important. While all the speeches were going on, people in the kitchen behind the curtains at the back of the stage were preparing food for afterwards. It was just nibbles and things, but the smell was overwhelming for Hatti and about five minutes into my speech, she got up from where she was lying to the left of the lectern and went off in search of a treat or ten. If I'm wearing trainers and a tracksuit when this happens (and I often am at these events), this is fine, but sometimes I'm required to wear something more formal (as was the case at this event), and when Hatti starts pulling on me without warning in mid-speech and I'm wearing heels, anything can happen. She's almost pulled me over before so, with this in mind, I usually try and attach her to something. On this occasion, I'd had to take my chances as there was nothing obvious to tie her to, but having smelled the food myself, I was ready for her! 'Not this time,' I said gently pulling her back towards the lectern. And it got a laugh from the audience, which was nice.

Anyway, back to Crufts. Apart from our antics on the Eukanuba stand, I remember signing a few autographs and very little else, besides marvelling at all the different dogs and owners and feeding Hatti treats by way of compensation for her having to deal with quite so much attention. There is one other thing I remember doing there though. At the time, I'd got it into my head that Hatti needed a companion and that her companion was going to be a miniature Dachshund. Because there were some miniature Dachshund breeders at the show, I decided to take Hatti to see what she thought of the idea. It didn't go well. She was aloof at best and I could tell within seconds that they weren't her kind of dog. I have to say, I was gutted at the time. In hindsight though, I'm very glad we didn't get one because I've since heard that miniature Dachshunds are generally very bossy, and the last thing Hatti and I needed was an overbearing canine gnome barking all the time and telling us what to do. Hatti would never have forgiven me.

Although the Dachshund decision didn't require rubber stamping, a few weeks later, Hatti and I went to another Eukanuba event, this time in Hyde Park. Just like Crufts, there were dogs running absolutely everywhere and the one making the most noise was a miniature Dachshund who appeared to be very protective over his newfound friends. For the two or three hours we were there, all you could hear was this tiny little dog barking at other dogs. It was a great day out though and despite everything I've said I still love the idea of getting a miniature-Dachshund. Don't tell Hatti! Or Dan. Or Elmo! Speaking of Elmo. I think it's time you were introduced.

CHAPTER EIGHT

ELMO MOVES IN

Elmo moving in resulted in one of the most worrying times I've ever had with Hatti. But before we talk about that, I've just realised I haven't even told you about Dan moving in, which happened first.

Dan moved in with me and Hatti shortly before the fox debacle at the bungalow. Although I wasn't required to, I ended up having a quick chat with Debbie from the Guide Dogs charity to see if she had any tips about a new partner moving into a home where a guide dog already lived. It turned out she didn't have any tips as such, but she did have a few stories about what can happen in that situation. I assumed they would be about the effect of the new resident on the guide dog, but was shocked to learn that almost all of them involved the partner being put out by the dog. Apparently, when a partner moves in, they want to be as helpful as possible, at least initially, and the relationship between a guide dog and its owner – which, at the end of the day, is based on help and assistance – can hinder that ambition. Dogs can certainly be quite random sometimes, but you know what they say: there's nowt so queer as folk.

Rightly or wrongly, if Hatti didn't like somebody, that would make me very wary, and I'd find it difficult to strike up a relationship with them, especially a close one. It would be the proverbial elephant in the room, if you like. It's rare that Hatti does take against somebody, and there isn't a particular 'type', but when it happens, she won't give them the time of day, which is unusual for her, and I find it very unnerving. She'll also stand very still or sit up very straight in their presence. I have no idea what she's sensing and, of course, it doesn't mean the person's not nice, but it's almost impossible to ignore, and that's down to how much I trust Hatti and how close we are. So, normally, and just to save trouble, if Hatti really takes against somebody, I'll try and limit the contact I have with them, which solves the problem. I also hate seeing her so uncomfortable, so it's the best course of action.

Hatti can also be very protective of me. I'll give you an example. After I'd split up with the boyfriend I was with before Dan, he came to the house one day to pick up some things. As can often happen in that situation, we got into an argument, and although it was nothing serious, he started shouting at one point. Until then, he and Hatti had always got on well, but the moment he raised his voice, her opinion began to change. I was sitting in a little armchair at the time and as soon as he shouted, Hatti jumped up on my knee. In all the time I'd had her, she'd never done anything like that. She also weighs about 30kg, so it was quite a surprise. My ex was just emotional at the time, so I didn't feel threatened, but Hatti didn't know that and once she was up on my knee, she refused to budge until he'd gone. It was a relief when he did leave as my legs were going numb!

The closest Hatti's ever come to that sort of behaviour since then is when Dan and I are playfighting. Because he does judo, Dan will sometimes pin me down and Hatti is quite puzzled by this. She'll start nipping at Dan's clothes, as if to say, 'That's as far as it goes, Dan. Just be careful!' And you can tell she's teetering on the precipice of leaping in and pulling him off me. Nevertheless, I'm still unsure if Hatti would save me if I ever was under attack. Especially if the attacker was brandishing a hot dog.

Anyway, what Dan had going for him when he moved in with us, at least in Hatti's eyes, was that he was somebody other than me. As I said earlier, the familiarity we have has never caused a problem between me and Hatti, and certainly no contempt – not in the slightest - but at the end of the day she's quite a sociable dog, so her day-to-day life might have been a bit humdrum and probably not as fulfilling as it could have been. And if I'm honest, it allowed me some space, too.

Just like me, Dan had to be coaxed slightly into applying for a guide dog, although, to be fair, he probably wasn't as bad as me. Dan used Hatti once or twice (although he's not supposed to), just very locally, and while they weren't necessarily suited, it gave him an idea of what it was like using a guide dog, which helped him make the decision. He had to wait longer than I did, but Guide Dogs found Dan a potential match relatively quickly and I remember arriving home one day to find that Elmo, who Dan had met once previously, had come to visit. The visit was with a view to Dan and Elmo being paired, following which Elmo would come to live with us, but because we already had Hatti, the people at Guide Dogs had to make sure that the house was big enough and that she wouldn't mind him being there.

When I arrived back, everyone was in the garden and the first thing I saw when I found them all was Hatti and Elmo running around together. In all the time I'd known her, I'd never seen Hatti as happy in another dog's company, so everyone was confident that if Elmo moved in with us everything would be ok.

Two weeks later, Elmo turned up with his carer from Guide Dogs. Dan had been out to buy him a new bed (one you could actually wash, fortunately) and some toys and they were due to start their training the following week. The only one of us who wasn't happy with the new arrival was Hatti, despite having been all over him two weeks previously. She'd started to behave oddly when the new bed appeared and then, when Elmo turned up, she must have put two and two together. Her first act of defiance was deciding that her bed was no longer nice enough and that only his new one would do. She must have thought that if she commandeered Elmo's bed, he'd just leave. She was going to be disappointed.

By the end of the first day, it must have become apparent to Hatti that Elmo was here to stay and she was not a happy bunny. Her second act of defiance was to pinch Elmo's toys; much to her annoyance though, he couldn't give a stuff. Elmo was just happy to be here and everything Hatti did was like water off a duck's back. Whenever Elmo came into the room Hatti would walk out, but the only one who lost in that situation was Hatti as she'd end up on her own. Dan and I tried our best to get her to come round, but short of teaching her English or us learning dog and explaining the situation calmly and concisely, we were at a loss. Not even food made a difference, which is when we knew we were in trouble.

The advice from Guide Dogs had been to concentrate on Dan and Elmo's relationship first, so that the two of them could consolidate their bond, and then worry about Hatti later. What became more of a worry, however, was *my* relationship with Elmo. This was far less important than his and Dan's, but because of what was happening with Hatti, I couldn't go anywhere near him or pay him any attention for fear of making things worse, so he must have thought I didn't like him.

As time went on, things just deteriorated. Hatti's tolerance of Elmo went from bad to non-existent and her behaviour went from being obstinate to downright strange. We had an idea from the off that she was probably jealous of Elmo, but what on earth could we do about it? The amount of attention she was getting from both of us was off the scale, yet it made no difference whatsoever. I joke about the food thing, but at the end of the day, it's Hatti's passion (or obsession) and the fact that she wasn't interested in any kind of edible incentives and was even going off her own food was incredible, and not in a good way.

It seemed to Dan and me that Hatti had gone into some kind of depression and the longer it went on, the more we worried about her. I felt so guilty. As I said, her behaviour was bizarre. Every night, about half an hour before bedtime, she'd go and lie by the back door. The first time she did it I thought she must have needed a wee, so I opened the door for her. But when she went outside, instead of going to the toilet, she just lay down on the concrete slabs. 'What are you doing there, Hatti?' I asked, walking over and giving her a stroke. 'Come inside.' What made this even stranger was that she was right next to the grass, which, bearing in mind it was quite cold, would have been a lot more comfortable. I was thinking about carrying her inside at one point, but wasn't sure how she'd react, so in the end, I just left her there. She eventually came in of her own accord around midnight and went straight to bed. The following night the same thing happened and it quickly became the norm. Even when it was raining, Hatti would go out and lie down on the cold concrete on her own, looking really miserable. Both Dan and I tried staying with her and stroking her, but it made no difference. She wasn't tense when we touched her. In fact, it was the opposite. It was as though she'd given up. It was awful.

The only time Hatti was happy during this period – or happier – was when she was working, presumably because she was away from Elmo. But coming back home in the evening became a nightmare. She knew the journey to and from the track very well and she also knew what each journey signified. The first one meant us arriving at the track and the second, at home. She was fine until I put her harness on her at the end of training, and I think sometimes she'd forget where we were going, but as the journey progressed, the realisation would slowly sink in, and she'd morph from being the Hatti I knew and loved into the Hatti I still loved but no longer knew. Watching her change like that, day after day, was heartbreaking. Dan, too, felt guilty for bringing Elmo into the house, but what was he supposed to do? We'd done everything in our power to make Hatti feel loved, happy and secure.

The first time Hatti arrived home after a day at the track was dreadful. I think she must have either forgotten about Elmo or was hoping he'd moved out. Until we got to the front door, she was ok, but when Dan opened the door for us and she saw Elmo I could feel her drop about an inch. All he wanted to do was say hello and play, but she wouldn't even look at him.

As well as ignoring Elmo as best she could or lying outside on the concrete in all weathers, Hatti would try to get one over on Elmo whenever possible. If he went into his bed, she'd chase him out – and God help him if he tried to use her bed instead. Everything he did was wrong in her eyes and she used every opportunity to let him know.

After four or five weeks, we were at the end of our tether. Even Elmo, usually the most laid-back dog on the planet, was starting to get upset all the time and it got to a point where each dog was constantly trying to avoid the other. Dan and I and the charity had run out of ideas and we were bordering on having to make a decision. Or at least I was. We couldn't go on like this for ever and something had to give. I didn't tell Dan at the time, but the only thing I could think of that would unquestionably have made a difference was for him and Elmo to move out and, for a time, I was definitely considering it. Of course, I didn't want that. But I was at my wits' end and wanted it all to stop.

Fortunately, that thought was put to bed when I received a phone call at the track one day from my sister, Felicity. As you might remember, Felicity is a veterinary nurse and she had taken a keen interest in what had been happening. We all knew the crux of the problem – Hatti feeling pushed out and jealous of Elmo – but we just didn't know what to do about it.

Like the rest of us, Felicity had come up with all kinds of suggestions, but nothing had made the slightest difference. 'I've had another idea,' she began this time. 'As opposed to trying to make Hatti feel she's as important as Elmo, I think you need to make her feel like she's still the top dog. After all, Hatti was there before him.'

At first, I was unsure as I thought it might create a hierarchy; but then Fliss reassured me there actually needs to be a hierarchy, as there would be in a normal pack. 'What do you have in mind?' I asked her. 'Try putting Hatti's bed in your bedroom for a night or two,' she suggested. 'If you do that, she'll definitely feel like number one. I honestly think it'll work.'

A few days before, I'd bought Hatti some new toys, but I hadn't yet given them to her. I wanted what we were about to do to involve all three of us, so while I took Hatti's bed into our room, Dan took out the toys and gave them to her. I'm not sure she knew what was going on at first, but the fact that we'd moved her bed into our room definitely sparked her interest. Instead of refusing the toys, as she would have done at any point prior to that, she took them from Dan, went to her bed and started playing with them. It was still early days, but we hadn't seen Hatti behave like this in well over a month.

Dan and I couldn't have got more than about four hours' sleep that night. Every ten minutes or so one of us would sit up slightly to see if there was any movement from Hatti. It was like having a newborn baby in the room.

We were both bleary-eyed the following morning, but Hatti's mood put a spring in our step. She wasn't back to normal by any stretch of the imagination, but rather than leaving the room when she saw Elmo, she stayed where she was and when she and I left for the track, I definitely saw her tail wag.

Because we were making progress with Hatti, we ended up keeping her bed in our room for about four nights, by which time she was back to normal. Now a hierarchy had been established she was fine because she knew she was top dog. When I say 'normal', she was back to how she had been prior to Elmo moving in, which, while amazing, still left the problem of whether the two of them could get on. As far as we were concerned, this was something that could be worked on over time and if it took a year, fine. The fact that we didn't have to worry about Hatti any more and that the two of them could at least tolerate each other was just the platform we needed.

Looking back, and having spoken to quite a few people about this, I think it's probably similar to what can happen when people have a second child. All children love getting attention and if a newer one comes along and starts taking the attention away from the firstborn, it's going to cause some resentment. Although Dan himself moving in had been fine, it was still a big change for Hatti and could easily have gone the other way had she not taken to him. I think Elmo moving in was probably a bridge too far for her initially, especially as he was another dog. Competition, basically.

To Elmo's credit, he was the one who did all the running after Hatti came round. He was just a little scared of her for a time, but once she was back to normal, he was ready to start working on her.

Whereas Hatti's obsession is food, Elmo's is snuggling, and whenever he saw Hatti lying down, he'd walk over and try and snuggle her. At first, Hatti was not interested at all, but instead of walking off into another room as she had previously, she'd just moved over and create some space between them. This, in itself, made us believe that if Elmo persisted, he'd get there eventually. And persist he did. If you could measure persistence in dogs, Elmo would be off the scale. The thing is, I think he actually enjoyed it. And Hatti certainly did. She may have been playing hard to get a lot of the time, but the fact that he was showing her love definitely began to register and, over time, she started moving away less and less.

The first time I noticed that Hatti had given in to Elmo's advances was about a year later, when we'd just moved to a new house. One morning, I walked into the living room and there, lying next to each other with no gap between them whatsoever, were Hatti and

Elmo. In fact, Hatti was lying on Elmo slightly. I remember saying something along the lines of, 'Thank God for that!' Later that day, I saw Hatti go and lie down next to Elmo of her own volition and then settle down and rest her head on his back. That was akin to a snuggle and was the ultimate gesture of acceptance. Since then, they've been as thick as thieves and do everything together.

That said, a pecking order has definitely developed, which is what I was fearful of, but rather than being overtly hierarchical, it's just a case of Hatti exerting her seniority from time to time. She does it very subtly, to be fair, and can even make Elmo think that he's in charge sometimes. I'm not sure if that's actually the case, but that's how it seems.

If Hatti could understand English and she heard me saying this, I'm sure she'd go spare, but when Dan goes away for a few days with Elmo, which he does quite often, Hatti definitely misses him. Elmo, that is, although I'm sure she misses Dan too. Once again, she's different at the track, as she forgets about everything else when she's there. The moment she gets home though and realises that Elmo's not there, she gets quite clingy with me and a bit sad. It's the absolute antithesis of what she used to be like when he first moved in, which is quite funny. When Dan and Elmo get home, I think Hatti knows that he's missed her just as much as she's missed him, and although she's desperate to give him love, she always lets him come to her. It's a woman's prerogative, I suppose.

What's also really sweet is that Hatti and Elmo love working together now, and if Dan or I ever go out on our own, then whichever dog is left behind won't be happy. If Dan's going out and I'm not, Hatti will try and go with him and Elmo, despite Dan not being able to work two dogs. It's the same when Hatti and I go out. The thing is, working in tandem with another dog is actually the norm as that's how guide dogs are trained. As I've already said, they're both very professional and although they enjoy working together, they're extremely focused. Elmo always enjoys being slightly in front of Hatti and fortunately Hatti doesn't mind that. If she did, can you imagine what would happen? Dan and I would be in a constant race.

Had you offered me, back at the very beginning of all this, the opportunity for Hatti and Elmo to just be in the same room together, tolerating each other, I'd have grabbed it with both hands. The fact that they're now basically best friends and we're all one big, happy family is more than we could ever have wished for. Long may it last.

CHAPTER NINE

HATTI'S PHOBIAS

Hatti was only two years old when she was paired with me, which meant there were still certain things that we didn't know about her, such as whether or not she had any phobias. Debbie mentioned when Hatti came to live with me that she wasn't keen on travelators or escalators, but I don't use them very much, so it went straight to the back of my mind. The fact that Debbie told me Hatti had once refused to get on to an escalator in return for a massive hot dog should have rung alarm bells though. Big ones.

Anyway, the problem didn't come to light until about two years after Hatti moved in with me, largely because if I have the choice between an escalator or travelator and stairs and, well, the floor, I'll always take the latter. At the end of the day, I'm an athlete and athletes tend to be quite active. In addition to that I'm a sprinter, so time is always of the essence. But eventually, just like buses, it turned out we had to use three in two days, and by the time we came off the third, Hatti was on the verge of a nervous breakdown and me a broken back.

The first time we came across a travelator was in Manchester Piccadilly train station. I was on my way to my grandparents' house, to stay with them for a week, and in addition to Hatti, I had a massive suitcase with me and a backpack. The travelator was linking two platforms and there was no walkway either side of it. In other words, it was the travelator or nothing. As Debbie's warning came back to me, I realised the next few minutes were going to be a test.

Would Hatti refuse altogether when confronted with a travelator or would she gingerly step on to it after a five-minute wait while a queue built up behind us? Either way, it had all the makings of something you'd see on an episode of *You've Been Framed*.

It was quite late at night and there was nobody else around, so at least I didn't have the problem of holding anybody up. As Hatti and I approached the travelator I could feel her slow down; by the time we were about half a metre away from it, she'd ground to a complete halt.

'What's up with you, Hatti?' I asked in as friendly and encouraging a way as possible. 'Come on, it's easy, really.' With that I took her back a few metres and tried a second time, but exactly the same thing happened. One thing I certainly wasn't going to do was try and force her on to the travelator, so the only option left open to me was to carry her. With a suitcase and a backpack this was easier said than done, but having chucked the suitcase on the travelator, I then picked up Hatti, who didn't seem to mind, stepped on and attempted to enjoy the ride.

As I said much earlier, one of the things we covered in training was how to lift Hatti up, although that was in the event of having to take her to the vet, not on a travelator. Thinking back, I must have looked like an absolute loon, carrying my guide dog. Then again, it was in the spirit of our relationship. She helps me, I help her.

I later learned that there's a flight of stairs just behind the travelator which we could have used instead. I was absolutely devastated when I found out.

The following day, we went shopping – this time without a suitcase and backpack – and after buying a couple of things in a department store, we made our way to the exit. I think we were on the fourth floor at the time and when we eventually got to the lifts, the queue was a mile long. Once again, I didn't see any stairs, and because the store was packed, I couldn't be bothered to ask where they were. There was only one thing for it, and we made our way over to the escalator which was also very busy. Emboldened by our travelator experience, I warned Hatti what was about to happen, walked her to the top step where she came to a halt, picked her up and stepped on. I didn't even give her a chance to walk on to it herself this time as it was so busy. Once again, she was a very happy passenger and on reaching the floor below, I put her down, walked with her to the next one and picked her up again. As you'd expect, we got some very funny looks from our fellow shoppers, but we didn't care. People often assume that I'm training Hatti, so if anyone asked, this was part and parcel. I was training her on how to avoid using escalators!

On the subject of training, a few weeks later, I did try coaxing Hatti on to a travelator, just in case there was any hope. I forget where we were, but it was very early in the morning and so, with nobody else around and a bag of dog treats in my pocket, I set to work. After walking Hatti right up to the very edge of the travelator – in itself a bit of a task – I put a treat on to it and stepped back. I don't think Hatti had even had her breakfast at this point, so she should have been ravenous. Even so, instead of stepping on to the travelator and devouring the treats as I'd hoped, Hatti just looked at them longingly, but didn't move a muscle. I knew that look though. I knew it all too well. She was definitely interested. Reaching into my pocket again, I pulled out three treats this time, put them on the travelator and stood back, expecting hunger to win the day. This time she didn't even look at them. I just could not believe it. I decided to give it one more roll of the dice and, after giving her one treat, which I hoped would whet her appetite, I gave her a little a pep talk, put six or seven more treats on the travelator and once again hoped for the best. This time, unbelievably, she just walked away in disgust. That was three times she'd turned down food which, in my mind, verified the phobia. This was real.

But back to shopping in Manchester. A couple of hours after I'd carried Hatti down the escalator in the department store, we came across another one. By this time, I had several bags with me, one of which weighed a tonne, and with the lifts being popular and no stairs in sight, I once again decided to go straight for plan C. The difference between this escalator and the previous one, however, was that it was about half as wide – something I only realised when I reached the top step. But with a queue of people behind me, I just had to go for it and hope for the best. I waited for the person in front of me to move down a step or two, literally threw my shopping on to the escalator, picked Hatti up and stepped on. Which is when I saw that not only was it narrow, we were also miles from the next level down. Normally, I couldn't give a monkey's about things like that, but because I was carrying Hatti, I have to confess to feeling a little bit wobbly for a while, especially at the top. I think Hatti must have sensed this because instead of feeling like a dead weight, as she had when I'd carried her earlier, she was now quite tense. She even gave me a couple of sideways glances as if to say, 'Are you sure you know what you're doing, mum?' It was a hairy ride and when we finally reached the bottom, I was probably in a worse state than she was.

I found out much later that it's thought one of the reasons why dogs don't like escalators or travelators – apart from the movement, which can have an effect on anyone – is the way the surface feels on their paws. I'm not sure this has been proven, but that's the theory and it seems quite plausible.

There was one other time when I had to lift Hatti, but this had nothing to do with her phobia. We were out walking when we came across a fence with a stile for humans to get over it, but nowhere for dogs to do so. We could have turned back, I suppose, but that would have been the same as giving in, and I wasn't about to do that. Hatti and I had a route and we were going to stick to it. One thing I didn't consider when making this decision was the fact that negotiating a stile that was probably getting on for five feet high with a 30kg dog in my arms and a backpack was a very different proposition from walking on to an escalator. Sure enough, the moment I tried to lift Hatti on to the first step, I knew I was in trouble, so I had to stand down and think again. Fortunately, just as I was thinking about how I was going to get her over, a man appeared on the other side and offered to take her from me if I lifted her up. This seemed like it was going to be our only chance, so having accepted the man's offer, I summoned up as much strength as I could, lifted Hatti up as far as possible and hoped for the best. Luckily, the man helping us was quite tall, so he was able to reach over the top of the stile and take Hatti from me, just as he'd suggested. I'm sure he winced though when he realised how heavy she was. To Hatti's credit, bearing in mind I was handing her over to a complete stranger and in mid-air, she was very well behaved and just accepted her fate. I did get another of her side-eyed glances though, so it hadn't gone unnoticed.

I'm so glad Guide Dogs showed me how to lift Hatti, otherwise it could have ended badly on at least one occasion.

Another quirk of Hatti's, albeit not exactly a phobia (although I'm sure she would tell you otherwise), is that if you take her past a branch of TK Maxx and she spots the sign outside, she'll instinctively try to walk in the opposite direction. I used to go there a lot with a friend of mine, until I gradually got to learn that it wasn't Hatti's favourite place. Or, I should say, that it was her least favourite place. That would be far more accurate.

Thinking about it now, I can totally understand why Hatti hates TK Maxx. For a start, it always seems to be full of stock and there are more rails than you can wave a stick at. Being about two feet tall must make it seem like a maze and I think she feels a bit stifled. I call it the London effect where Hatti's concerned, and even though it took me a little while to catch on (I was always too busy trying things on to notice, I'm afraid), I'm wise to it now and will always try to make sure she's got plenty of space in which to move and see. Especially in a clothes shop.

Another reason why Hatti developed an allergic reaction to TK Maxx is because my friend and I used to spend hours in there, so Hatti's patience was tested to the absolute max. Or should I say Maxx.

To compensate for this torture, I used to allow Hatti to do the leading after we'd left, so we'd go wherever she wanted to. Depending on which town or city centre we were in – usually either Loughborough or Leicester – she'd take me to whichever café she'd received the most treats and affection at previously and finding it was never a problem. Armies aren't the only things that march on their stomachs. What was a problem, however, was stopping Hatti from just wandering straight in and basically demanding food.

One of her favourite eateries was in Nottingham, and regardless of whether she'd had to stand around in TK Maxx for several hours or not, I'd always let her take me there at some point during the day. I often used to go to a gym in Nottingham, and because that, too, involves a certain amount of waiting around on Hatti's part, her treat on the way home was to turn left up a little alleyway where, at the very end, is said favourite eatery: a dog-friendly café with a seemingly inexhaustible supply of dog treats that customers can help themselves to. Within reason.

Whenever we go there, the first question they always ask me is, Who's driving today? You or Hatti? And it's usually Hatti. But it's not just food outlets that Hatti makes a beeline for. It's basically anywhere she's been made a fuss of. Sometimes she'll see somebody she likes going into a shop and if I'm not concentrating, the next thing I know, we'll be going in after them. That doesn't happen very much during daylight hours as there are usually lots of people around, so I tend to have my wits about me. In the evening, however, it's a different matter. Hatti has no idea about things like opening hours, so if she's feeling hungry on the way home, she'll sometimes take us on a detour to a little café she knows. It'll probably only be a minute or two off our route, which is why I don't realise sometimes, and I'll only come round once we're standing at the door. The café in question is obviously closed, but Hatti has no idea and just looks at me expectantly. Come on then, she's thinking. Let's go in!

Hatti is led by her stomach and a sense of intuition, so if I'm not concentrating and she takes us off somewhere, I just have to deal with it – it's my own fault. But this can prove potentially dangerous sometimes: one night, I came to my senses in a wooded area and just for a moment I didn't know where the hell we were. At that moment, I started panicking as I thought we might get attacked, but we were ok in the end. Once again, we were only a minute or two from our homeward route, but Hatti must have picked up the scent of some fox poo or something. And if Hatti gets a sniff of fox poo, that's it.

One of the most frustrating things that happens to Hatti and me in daylight – and this isn't my fault, for a change – is when Hatti decides that she wants to play hide and seek. This isn't just a metaphor for her running off and enjoying herself. She actually goes off and hides from me and I have to try and find her. She only does this when I've taken her on a free walk, but if we're in a big space, it can be a nightmare finding her. I do sometimes, though, and she always gets very excited. Sometimes when I've spotted Hatti, I'll shout for her to come to me, but if *she* hasn't seen *me* and thinks I'm still looking for her, she'll stand very, very still. Fortunately, she has the attention span of a five-year-old, so if I haven't found her after about five or ten minutes, she'll come bounding out from her hiding place. She sometimes stands still when she runs into a stream, too, so it's not exclusive to a game of hide and seek. It might be because the water's cold, but she'll just stand there for a few minutes as if she's playing musical statues.

Hatti's second proper phobia is fireworks. It's an obvious one where dogs are concerned, yet when Hatti first came to live with me, she didn't have a problem with them. It all went wrong about a year and a half ago. I let Hatti out for a wee shortly before bed one night and she was halfway through when a firework went off. Had it been around bonfire night or Christmas, I doubt she would have minded, but this was right out of the blue. (Loughborough is full of students and if they get their hands on a few fireworks, regardless of the time of year, they're going to let them off.)

Poor Hatti was absolutely terrified. Then again, if I was sitting on a loo outdoors and a firework went off unexpectedly, I think I might be taken aback, too. Since then, whenever she hears fireworks, she'll immediately start shaking. If I'm sitting on the sofa, she'll jump straight up and ask for a cuddle; if I'm asleep, she'll come into our bedroom and wake me up. It's that bad.

In 2020, because people weren't able to go to any official firework displays due to Covid, there were a lot more random fireworks going off in people's gardens, so it was a bad year for Hatti (not to mention the millions of other dogs who are scared of them). As a consequence, I had to be very careful about when and where I worked Hatti around bonfire night and Diwali, making sure we were back indoors by about 5 pm. The thought of Hatti being outside when there are fireworks going off everywhere fills me with dread, as does the thought of her being at home on her own. If we're ever unlucky enough to be out when there are fireworks going off, Hatti will start dictating the pace and, in that situation, I just let her get on with it.

On a slightly brighter note, Elmo, who really doesn't give a monkey's about fireworks, yet is a world-class attention seeker, will often use them as an opportunity to put on a performance. For instance, if he and Hatti are outside in the garden and somebody lets off a firework, Hatti will immediately come running to the door to be let in. Elmo, on the other hand, who is always in a world of his own, will carry on playing – until he realises that Hatti is getting some attention. The moment that happens, Elmo will turn from being a happy-go-lucky dog enjoying himself in the garden into a gibbering wreck who desperately needs attention *now*. 'And the Oscar for best canine performance in a garden with a few fireworks going off in the background goes to . . . Elmo!'

To help Hatti's phobia (and to prevent Elmo from doing his dying-swan act all the time), I invested in some plug-in things that give off a smell that's supposed to help calm dogs down. You're meant to plug them in about a week before you think the fireworks might start (although it's not an exact science), but at some point in between me plugging them in and the fireworks starting in earnest, somebody called Dan, thinking they were air fresheners, systematically unplugged them, so he could charge his laptop and phone. Consequently, when the fireworks started, Hatti was still scatty and Elmo was still Elmo and, in the end, I didn't bother plugging them back in again. Bonfire night was now upon us and we just had to make do. They were about £40 each though!

A potential dilemma I'll have going forward is what to do if and when Edward wants to go and see a display. I don't think I've ever met a child who doesn't like fireworks and his love of bright colours and loud noises gives me the feeling that he'll be a big fan. That said, last bonfire night, Edward was not keen; but having said that, we *were* stuck indoors, so instead of being able to see them he could only hear the bangs. This meant that in addition to a black Labrador cross clinging on to me for dear life all evening, I also had a small child. And it didn't get any better at bedtime. The students at Loughborough University don't care what time of day or night it is and the fireworks went off all through the night. Neither Hatti nor Edward settled and so that was it for me. Thank God Elmo wasn't here as that would have been too much!

The only other thing Hatti's unsure of, although I wouldn't necessarily class it as a phobia, is swimming. I'm not even sure if she can swim, to be honest, as I've certainly never seen her. I've seen her run into water literally hundreds of times, but she never goes in above her belly.

As far as I know, that's not normal, especially for a Labrador Retriever cross. They're like fish with legs, usually. As I said, she's not nervous around water – she's just very sensible. I have tried coaxing her into slightly deeper water, just as I've tried coaxing her on to a travelator. I assumed that her unease stemmed from the fact that she'd simply never experienced it before, and that once she was in a bit deeper, she'd start swimming like other dogs. I even followed the same principle as I tried with treats on the travelator, in that when I was throwing stones for her, I'd try throwing them a little further, where the water was deeper, in the hope that she'd run after them. But just like the travelator treats, the stones were left where they landed, so I just gave up in the end.

One theory I have has to do with her fur, which holds water quite well, so probably makes her feel heavy. That would make me feel nervous about going into deep water, too. Hatti also takes a very long time to dry when she gets wet, whereas Elmo, who loves swimming, dries in a few minutes.

Speaking of Elmo, he has a very strange phobia. Or at least I think it's strange. He hates boxes and bags. If Dan's walking with him and he has a shopping bag in his other hand, Elmo will become very scatty and uneasy, constantly looking behind him to see where the bag is. Perhaps he was hit by a bag with something in it once, but I'm not sure.

I remember one time, before we had Edward, Dan and I and Hatti and Elmo were walking home from the shops. Between us, Dan and I were carrying about ten carrier bags and we must have forgotten that they're Elmo's nemesis. The journey home was one of the most bizarre ever, as poor Elmo clearly thought he was under attack. He spent almost the entire walk looking behind him until, in the end, we had to try and hide the bags behind our backs to make him believe they'd gone. We must have looked very strange.

Whereas Hatti's a fairly typical dog (despite not being a swimmer), Elmo is anything but. As a guide dog, he's incredibly professional: the moment you put a harness on him he's Mr Guide Dog and for as long as he's got it on, he will not deviate from that role. Take his harness off, however, and he's a loose cannon – if you met him off duty, you'd think he'd escaped from a doggy lunatic asylum. What we've discovered – and I alluded to this earlier – is that Elmo's behaviour off the harness is all about getting attention, so the more you give him, the less he acts up. The only problem with this is that it can take up a lot of time, so unless you're prepared to indulge him pretty much constantly, you have to bite the bullet and just let him get on with it. Come to think of it, it's exactly the same with humans. We all know people who thrive on attention and have to learn how to handle them.

Elmo had been paired with somebody prior to Dan, but they weren't able to cope with his personality off the harness. Perhaps they couldn't find a dressing room that was big enough? Anyway, it was touch and go at one point as to whether Elmo would have to be retired, but luckily, Dan came along. He and Elmo are as close as Hatti and me, and they're so well suited. One's an over emotional scatterbrain who loves attention, and the other's Elmo!

If there's one thing Hatti knows, it's her own mind and her limitations. I'd never do more than try gently to coax her into doing something she didn't want to – and even then, only if I thought she might benefit from it. Given the fact that she's put on a bit of lockdown lard (haven't we all) going on a diet might be on the cards soon, but she definitely won't like that!

CHAPTER TEN

RIO PART I

Before I talk about Rio, I must just tell you about Hatti's she-
nanigans at the track. It's quite a bold statement, but I think
Hatti has probably spent more time at athletics tracks than any
other dog on earth. Some people might think that's an exciting
prospect, but after a while, the novelty wears off and in Hatti's
case, I'm pretty sure it was never even there in the first place.
I mean, why would it be? Lot's of people running and jumping
and not a treat in sight. Whoopee!

Having arrived at the track, Hatti will find a nice heap of bags
somewhere – which are usually black, thus rendering her almost
invisible to me – and settle in for a nice sleep. You'd think that
with starting guns going off all the time she'd be disturbed, or
even frightened. Not a bit of it. For some reason, starting guns
don't really bother Hatti and I've seen her sleep through them
when they're going off just yards away. It's the same in the gym.
As with the starting gun, the noise of the weights clanging and

banging doesn't seem to affect her at all and when I'm training, she'll just find a corner somewhere and go to sleep. Every twenty minutes or so she'll appear suddenly – never when I'm lifting, fortunately – and demand a quick cuddle. Once she's had one, she'll loll off back to the pile of bags and coats she's been keeping warm and that'll be it for another twenty.

Something that piques Hatti's interest slightly more than a noisy starting gun or looking on while I lift weights or run is watching me and the other athletes do sprint-start sessions. This is the bit leading up to the starting gun being fired, and for some reason, it triggers a lot of excitement and anticipation within Hatti. She knows when it's going to happen, and as we're all getting ready on the start line, she'll stand up and start trotting around in a circle. Then, once we take our marks, she gets ready to run with us.

But as soon as the starting gun goes off, it's as though somebody has just sat on her back and she flops on to the floor. She's actually tied up at the time, so couldn't run with us anyway. This is essential at the track, as if Hatti was off the lead, she would indeed try and run with me, at least some of the time. I have enough trouble trying not to fall over her at home, let alone at the track.

Hatti is a fantastic guide dog, but I'm not sure she'd be much of a guide runner, if you see what I mean. I can just imagine it: you'd have three athletes with their respective guide runners all racing along in their lanes and then, right at the back, there'd be me desperately trying to stop Hatti from jumping up at me. That's what she always does when we have a run together in the park on a Sunday. In all seriousness, it is something I have to be very careful about; a few years ago, a blind athlete got completely taken out by her guide dog when the dog broke free of its lead one day during a race and, after running across the infield, it ran on to the track and ploughed into her. The athlete ended up suffering quite a few injuries. I couldn't in a million years imagine Hatti doing this (not unless I was covered in dog food), but she would probably try and run with me at certain points, so – for all our sakes – she has to stay tied up.

This has just reminded me of a story involving Elmo. A few years ago, Dan and Elmo were at a track meeting and Elmo was attached to Dan's bag. Normally, this would prevent a dog from running off, but as soon as Dan started his warm-up lap, Elmo got to his feet and started running after him. One of the athletes who wasn't racing had to run after Elmo and bring him back, and luckily, disaster was averted.

This story, in turn, reminds me of another involving Elmo. Only this time he did take somebody out – me! It happened shortly after Edward was born. Each Sunday, we'd always take a walk in the park and, would you believe it, across the road from there was a branch of Greggs, which I frequented. While Dan looked after the dogs and Edward, I'd pop off to get us a few treats. On this occasion, Dan was sitting on a bench holding Edward when I set off; but Hatti and Elmo ran after me. Dan called them both back but only Hatti did as she was told. According to Dan, Elmo half went back, then changed his mind, and just as I turned around to see if he'd listened, he went straight through my legs and took me clean out. Because he was so close, I didn't even see him and so it took me completely by surprise. Dan must have been a good fifty metres away, so he didn't see what had happened. Elmo had knocked me flat on my face, and thinking it was some kind of game, he and Hatti ran up to where I was lying and started running around and over me. It felt like they were mocking me, to be honest. The reason it happened is because Elmo genuinely doesn't know his own strength, bless him, so rather than getting angry, I let him off with a caution.

If I'm training at the indoor track, as I do in the winter, I'll sometimes let Hatti off the lead after I've finished. Then, a few of us will chase her around and play tig with her for a while. She'll also do a cool-down lap with us sometimes which is nice, although she rarely does the full lap. The only thing we have to be a bit careful of is the sandpit, as Hatti seems to think it's a doggie toilet, and over the years, we've had one or two close shaves. The only time Hatti *has* had a poo at the indoor track was quite memorable. Once again, I'd let her off the lead, so it was after a training session had finished. I was sitting chatting to some of the other athletes when, all of a sudden, I got a whiff of something. Something not very nice. My instinct was to say, 'Oh my God, I think Hatti's had a poo somewhere,' but in the interests of not drawing attention to the possibility, I decided to keep quiet and see if I could find and remove the offending article ASAP.

After excusing myself for a moment, I got up to go and investigate but by this time, the smell had reached my colleagues and they were all in on the job, so to speak. 'Ok, let's go and find it,' one of them said, and with that, they all stood up. Before we could even take a step, somebody said, 'I can see it,' and then started to giggle. Within about a second everybody else there was giggling, too, and when I looked in the direction they were pointing, I could just make out why. There, on the home straight, slap bang in the middle of the track, was a neat little pile of Hatti's poo. 'Oh my God,' I screamed. 'She's pooed on the bloody track!' Because this was a first, and because I wasn't quite sure how people would react, I ran off and got it cleaned up as soon as I could, all the time muttering apologies to everyone within earshot and assuring them it had never happened before, nor would it again. Hatti was fast asleep by this point. She'd done her bit!

Anyway, let's pop to Brazil, shall we?

My first long separation from Hatti – as in, over two weeks – was in 2016, when I went to compete at the Paralympic Games in Rio. I know this is supposed to be a book about me *and* Hatti but this is quite a good story, so I hope you'll indulge me for a few pages. Incidentally, Hatti had a ball while I was away and put her time to good use. All will be revealed.

My trip lasted just over four weeks and included two weeks at an acclimatisation camp in a city called Belo before we moved to the athletes' village, situated just outside Rio.

People have asked me why I didn't take Hatti with me. Well, apart from the flight, which would have been horrendous for her, there was also the weather. Despite it being the autumn over there when the Games were on, autumn in Rio is very, very different to autumn in Loughborough, and although I couldn't say for sure, I had the feeling that Hatti would have spent the majority of the month feeling uncomfortable. Don't get me wrong, I'd have loved to have taken her with me, but if I had, it would have been for my benefit only.

Another reason why I didn't take Hatti was because while I was away, I had my guide runner Chris Clarke to help me. It sounds daft, but because we spent so much time together, he did become a substitute for Hatti (minus the harness, the treats, the curious occasional smells and going to the toilet outside). In all seriousness though, my relationship with Chris is built on the same fundamentals as my relationship with Hatti, in that it's trust-based and every inch a partnership. I also get on very well with him, and as well as being a very talented athlete, he also makes me laugh, which helps.

One of the things that makes me laugh most about Chris is that he's probably one of the most easily distracted people I know. Just as Hatti gets distracted by squirrels and food a great deal, Chris gets distracted by everything. In conversation, Chris will suddenly veer off on to another subject without warning and you'll be left thinking, What on earth happened there? I've no idea how he manages to stay on the track.

Rio was my third Paralympic Games, yet despite me being more established than I had been prior to the other two, the run-up this time had been far more difficult. In fact, had you

Left: Hatti and me at Saffron Lane Athletics track, Leicester. We're having a post-race cuddle.

Below: Hatti and Elmo's first outing together. They're definitely ready to chase a ball.

Dan, Elmo and Hatti having a cuddle on the floor at home.

Hatti sunbathing at the track while she waits for me to finish training at Loughborough University's Paula Radcliffe Stadium.